W. D. Lighthall

**Montreal after 250 years**

W. D. Lighthall

**Montreal after 250 years**

ISBN/EAN: 9783742840981

Manufactured in Europe, USA, Canada, Australia, Japa

Cover: Foto ©ninafisch / pixelio.de

Manufactured and distributed by brebook publishing software (www.brebook.com)

W. D. Lighthall

**Montreal after 250 years**

This is a reproduction of a book from the McGill University Library collection.

Title: Montreal after 250 years
Author: Lighthall, W. D. (William Douw), 1857-1954
Publisher, year: Montreal : F.E. Grafton, 1892

The pages were digitized as they were. The original book may have contained pages with poor print. Marks, notations, and other marginalia present in the original volume may also appear. For wider or heavier books, a slight curvature to the text on the inside of pages may be noticeable.

ISBN of reproduction: 978-1-926748-61-0

This reproduction is intended for personal use only, and may not be reproduced, re-published, or re-distributed commercially. For further information on permission regarding the use of this reproduction contact McGill University Library.

McGill University Library
www.mcgill.ca/library

*Paul de Chomedey.*
*De Maisonneuve*

FONDATEUR DE MONTRÉAL 1642

# MONTREAL AFTER 250 YEARS

## BY W. D. LIGHTHALL, M.A.

MONTREAL: PUBLISHED BY F. E. GRAFTON & SONS AT THEIR BOOKSTORE, 250 ST. JAMES STREET. 1892.

Entered according to Act of Parliament of Canada, in the year eighteen hundred and ninety-two, by F. E. GRAFTON & SONS, in the Office of the Minister of Agriculture.

"WITNESS" PRINTING HOUSE,
MONTREAL.

DEDICATED

TO THE

### Numismatic and Antiquarian Society of Montreal:

MY FRIENDS AND FELLOW-STROLLERS

IN PLEASANT FIELDS.

## PREFACE.

The present description of Montreal is written in view of the erection, by the Numismatic and Antiquarian Society, of a number of historical tablets of marble, marking spots of special connection with the past. As a setting, a general account of the city was thought desirable, both for the information of strangers and to act as a record for the citizens. The text of the chief tablet inscriptions is given, and the object has been to make a readable volume, not too heavily encumbered with statistics, and presenting particularly the romance and interest of the town.

# LIST OF CONTENTS.

## PART I.

CHAPTER I.—History of the Site.
  II.—General Descriptive Outlines of the City.
  III.—Squares, Parks and Cemeteries.
  IV.—Public Buildings, Churches.
  V.—Charitable and Religious Institutions, Universities, Sports, Theatres, Clubs, etc.

## PART II.

Historical and Legendary.
Index.
Principal Authorities, etc.

## LIST OF ILLUSTRATIONS.

|   | PAGE |
|---|---|
| Portrait of Maisonneuve | *Frontispiece.* |
| Plan of Town of Hochelaga | 4 |
| Montreal from Tower of Notre Dame | *Facing* 8 |
| Victoria Bridge | " 14 |
| C.P.R. Bridge | " 18 |
| Seminary of St. Sulpice | 30 |
| Victoria Square | *Facing* 34 |
| Château de Ramezay | 38 |
| Y.M.C.A. Building | 40 |
| Windsor Hotel and Dominion Square | 43 |
| Lachine Rapids | 47 |
| Montreal from Mount Royal | *Facing* 50 |
| St. Gabriel Church | 64 |
| Old Seminary Towers | 90 |
| Montreal Fifty Years Ago (six illustrations) | *Facing* 100 |
| Plan of Ville-Marie, 1680 | " 108 |
| Plan of Montreal, 1759 | " 136 |

# Montreal after 250 Years.

### HISTORY OF THE SITE.

DIEDRICH KNICKERBOCKER approaches the subject of the Dutch history of New York with such respectful awe, that he commences his narrative at the beginning of the World! We, too, will go far back, and say that the original site of Montreal, some hundred million years ago, was the muddy bottom of a wide gulf or sea; of which mud, and of the fishes swimming above it, the crisp grey stone of her public buildings, her warehouses and her residences is the nineteenth-century form.

Her next shape was that of an immense and lofty volcano-peak, energetically puffing out its thick smoke, its molten lava and its showers of cinders—a busier spot than it has ever been since, yet an excellent advance notice of the manufacturing metropolis it was its intention to be, after getting duly pared down to a mere core by the great ice-movements of glacial ages, and then covered over with grass, trees, Indians, white men and real estate agents.

From time immemorial there was a town here. History opens with one in full view.

When Jacques Cartier, the Columbus of Canada, sailed up to the Island in 1535, having heard reports of a great Town and Kingdom of Hochelaga, he found a race of Indians living by a rude agriculture and fishing, who dwelt in a walled village containing some 1,500 souls.

These facts, taken with their language, of which he gives a list of words, and with their condition of peace, tend to show that they were of a race which at some time split into those two bitterly hostile nations, the Hurons and the Iroquois. The latter are better known outside of Canada as the Five Nations of New York, or, with the Tuscaroras of Florida afterwards added, the Six Nations.

## Aboriginal Traditions.

There are two legends of the cause of the dissension. One goes that a certain chief refused to permit his son to marry a particular maiden. She was a beauty, and swore never to favor any brave but he who should kill that chief. A warrior did so, and won her. But the race took sides in the feud, and hence arose the long, relentless war between the two peoples.

The other story is that the Algonquins, arrogant, nomadic hunters of a different tongue, subdued that part of the quieter, corn-planting race afterwards called Hurons, and induced them to join in oppressing the Iroquois. The latter were forced to apply their talents to the art of war, and did so with such success that, by means of their celebrated confederacy (which they called "The Chain"), they were about to conquer both the Hurons and Algonquins at the period of the arrival of Champlain.

There appears to have been more than one Indian village on the Island. Besides the cultivated space noticed around the Town of Hochelaga by Jacques Cartier, Champlain found about sixty acres which had once been tilled in the neighborhood of the present Custom House. It is recorded also that in 1642 certain Indians, called by the writer Algonquins (but who were probably not), exclaimed, with a kind of melancholy pride, to the French of Ville Marie during a pilgrimage to the top of Mount Royal : "We are of the nation of those who formerly inhabited this isle. Behold the spots where there were once towns filled with many Indians. Our enemies drove out our forefathers, and so this Island has become desert and without inhabitant."

An old man among them said that his grandfathers had lived there and cultivated the ground. "See," he said, taking up a handful of earth: "The soil is good, examine it!" Père Lalemant, the Jesuit missionary, writes, in 1656, that under the Algonquin name the French included a diversity of small peoples, among whom was one named **Ononchataronons, or the tribe of Iroquet,** "whose ancestors formerly inhabited the Island of Montreal, and who seem to have some desire to repossess it as their country." Again: "An old man, aged, say, 80 years, retired to Montreal. 'Here,' said he, 'is my country: my mother told me that in her

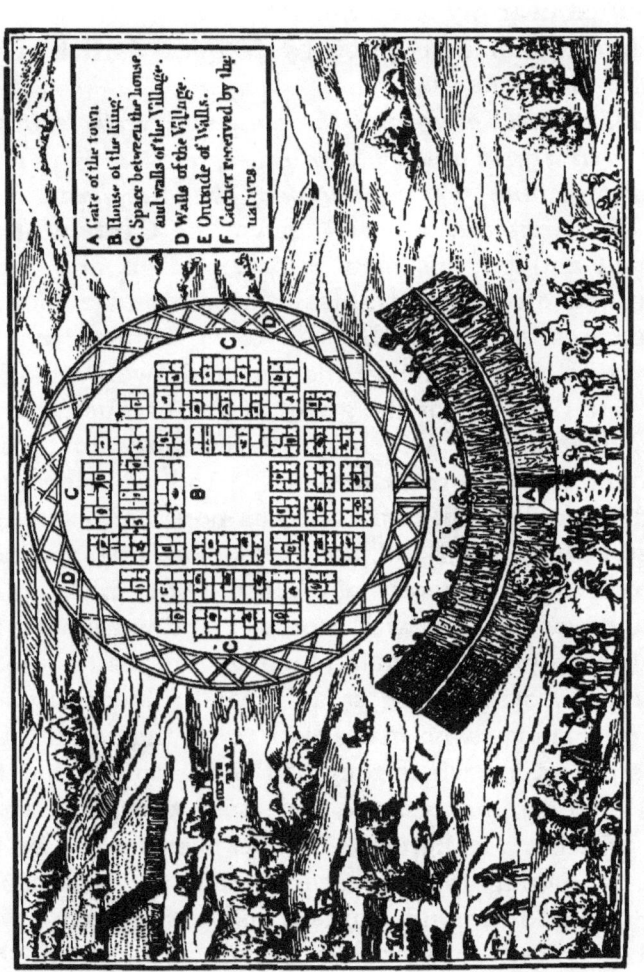

PLAN OF THE TOWN OF HOCHELAGA, 1535.

youth, the Hurons drove us from this Island: I wish to be buried near my forefathers.'"

The original description by Jacques Cartier of what he saw is as follows:

*"How the Captain and the gentlemen, with twenty-five men, well armed and in good order, went to the Town of Hochelaga, and of the situation of the said place.*

"The next day at early dawn the Captain arrayed himself and put his men in order, to go and see the town and dwelling of the said people, and a mountain which is adjacent to the said town, whither went with the said Captain the gentlemen and twenty mariners, and left the rest for the guard of the barques, and took three men of the said town of *Hochelaga* to take and conduct them to the said place. And we being on the road found it as beaten as it was possible to see, in the most beautiful soil and the finest plain: oaks as fair as there are any in forest of France, under which all the ground was covered with acorns. And we, having gone about a league and a half, found on the road one of the principal Lords of the said Town of Hochelaga with several persons, who made sign to us that we must rest there near a fire which they had made on the said road. And then commenced the said Lord to make a sermon and preaching, as hereinbefore has been told to be their way of making joy and acquaintance in making that Lord dear to the said Captain and his company, which Captain gave him a couple of axes and knives, with a Cross and a reminder of the Crucifix, which he made him kiss and hung at his neck: whereof he returned thanks to the Captain. That done, we walked on further, and about a half league thence we commenced to find the lands tilled and fair large fields full of corn of their lands, which is like Brazil rice, as large, or more, than peas, whereof they live as we do on wheat. And in the midst of those fields is situated and fixed the said Town of Hochelaga, near and joining a mountain which is in its neighborhood, well tilled and exceeding fertile; therefrom one sees very far. We named that mountain *Mont Royal.* The said town is quite round and palisaded with wood in three rows, in form of a pyramid, interlaced above, having the middle row in perpendicular, then lined with wood laid along, well joined and corded in their mode, and it is of the height of about two lances. And there is in that town but one gate and entrance, which shuts with bars, on which and in several places on said palisade is a kind of galleries, with ladders to mount them, which are furnished with rocks and stones for the guard and defence thereof. There are in that town about fifty houses each at most about fifty paces long and twelve or fifteen paces wide, all made of wood, covered and furnished in great pieces of bark as large as tables, well sewed artificially after their manner; and in them are several halls and chambers; and in the middle of said houses is a great hall on the ground, where they make their fire and live in common; then they retire to their said chambers, the men with their wives and children. And likewise, they have granaries above their houses where they put their corn, whereof they make their bread they call *Caraconi.* . . . . This people devote themselves only to tillage and fishing, to live: for they make no account of the goods of this life, because they have no knowledge of them, and do not leave their country, and are not wandering like those of *Canada* and *Saguenay*, notwithstanding that the said Canadians are subject to them, together with eight or nine other peoples who are on the said River."

The Hochelagans made much of Cartier, and brought him into the middle of their town to the public square, which was, he says, a good stone's throw from side to side. All the women kissed him, weeping for joy. The men then sat in order around, and the Agouhanna, or "lord and king of the country," was brought in on men's shoulders, wearing a porcupine head-dress. He was about fifty years old and palsied, and begged Cartier to touch and cure him. All the other sick also did so. He recited the first words of the Gospel of St. John, made the sign of the cross, and opening a service-book, read to them the entire passion of Christ, to which they attended gravely. He made a distribution of presents, and on leaving was taken to the top of Mount Royal, "about a quarter of a league from the town," where he was delighted with the view. After getting some rude geographical information from the people, he returned to his boats accompanied by a great multitude of them, who, when they saw any of his men weary, would take them on their shoulders and carry them on.

The Town of Hochelaga is one of the mysterious mirages of history, for, large though it was, it thenceforth completely disappears from record, with all its dusky warriors, its great square and its large maize fields. The very spot on which it stood—nearly in front of McGill Grounds on Sherbrooke Street, towards Metcalfe—was unknown until a few years ago, when it was accidentally re-discovered. In the words of one of those who took part:

"The memory of the place had remained forgotten for three hundred years, until, Herculaneum-like, it was discovered by men excavating for foundations. First a skeleton was brought to light in a sitting posture, then other skeletons; then specimens of pottery. On a more careful search being made by local antiquarians, the rubbish-heap of the town was found. This consisted of broken pottery and pipes, with bones of the animals used as food, besides the fragments of other items in their bill of fare. Much of the habits of the old townspeople was gathered from these researches. But the whole work was desultory, being left to the caprice of individuals. So far only the western border was touched upon—that by the brook, which, running through McGill College Grounds, passed down by Metcalfe Street." *

A tablet on the latter street, near Sherbrooke, marks the place where most of the relics were found, and reads as follows: "Site of a large Indian village, claimed to be the Town of Hochelaga visited by Jacques Cartier in 1535."

## La Place Royale.

The next white man to visit the Island was Samuel de Champlain, founder and first Governor of Canada, in 1611. He reached here, with an Indian and a French-

---

* R. W. McLachlan, Esq.

MONTREAL FROM THE TOWER OF NOTRE DAME CHURCH,

man, on the 28th of May, and, struck with the site, selected it at once for a city.

"After having moved about in one direction and another," he says, "as well in the woods as along the shore, to find a place suitable for the site of a dwelling whereon to prepare a spot for building, I walked eight leagues, skirting the great rapids, through the woods, which are open enough, and came as far as a lake to which our Savage led me, where I considered the country very closely. But, in all that I saw, I found no place more suitable than a little spot, which is as far as barques and boats can easily come up, unless with a strong wind or by a circuit, because of the great current; for higher than that place (which I named La Place Royale), a league away from Mount Royal, there are quantities of small rocks and ledges, which are very dangerous. And near the said Place Royal there is a little river which goes some distance into the interior, all along which there are more than sixty acres of deserted land, which are like meadows, where grain can be sown and gardens made. Formerly the savages tilled these, but they abandoned them on account of the wars they had there.

"Having, therefore, made particular examination and found this place one of the most beautiful on that river, I immediately had the wood cut and cleared away from the said Place Royale to make it even and ready for building, and anyone can pass water around it easily and make a little isle of it, and settle down there as he desires.

"There is a little island twenty rods from the said Place Royale, which is over 100 paces long, where one could make a good and strong dwelling. There is also much meadow-land of very good rich pottery clay, as well for brick as for building, which is a great convenience. I made use of a part of it, and built a wall there four feet thick and three to four high and ten rods long to test how it would keep during winter when the waters descend, which, in my opinion, would not come up to said wall, seeing that the bank is elevated twelve feet above said river, which is high enough. In the middle of the river there is an island about three-quarters of a league in circuit, fit for the building of a good and strong town, and I named it the Isle of Saincte Heleine. The rapids come down into a sort of lake, where there are two or three islands and fine meadow-lands.

"While awaiting the Savages, I there made two gardens, one in the meadows and the other in the woods, which I cleared, and the second day of June I sowed some grains, which all came up in perfection and in a short time, demonstrating the goodness of the ground.'

When we approach the neighborhood where he landed, and remember that the city was planned and even begun by so grand a man, the honor of his name and his character throws for us its halo about the place.

The fascinating story of the ultimate foundation of the city will be told in succeeding pages.

## CHAPTER II.

### GENERAL DESCRIPTIVE OUTLINES OF THE CITY.

THE **leading characteristics** of the Montreal of to-day are:
    Its magnificent situation,
    Its historic riches,
    Its commercial activity,
    The cosmopolitan charm of its division of languages and populations. It is, in this respect, the Alexandria of the West.

Few cities, if any, surpass it in **situation.** Past it, in front, sweeps the stately River of Rivers, the St. Lawrence, two miles in breadth, bearing down to the Gulf one-third of the fresh waters of the globe; in rear rises Mount Royal, its sides clothed with foliage, its recesses full of beautiful drives and views; and round about the city lies the extensive and fertile Island of Montreal, thirty-two miles long by nine wide, bordered with a succession of lovely bays, hamlets and watering-places. **Commercially,** the town is, and has always been, the metropolis of Canada. Seated at the head of ocean navigation, its sway as such extends over by far the largest portion of North America. Its connections have a notable influence on the western trade of the United States. It is backed by the great lake and canal system, which connects it with Chicago, Duluth and the cities of the interior of the continent, to which some day, by a short and easy cut, will, no doubt, be added those of the Mississippi. It is the headquarters of, among others, two of the greatest of railways—the Canadian Pacific, which runs from the Atlantic to the Pacific Oceans, and is the longest in the world, and its rival, the Grand Trunk. Its population, with the adjuncts which properly form part of it, amounts to a little under 300,000 souls, rapidly increasing. Though 620 miles from the sea, Montreal is a great seaport.

Looking around from the top of the towers of Notre Dame, one might say to himself: "This city is the Mother of the cities of the West. Yonder was the birthplace of the founder of New Orleans, the home of La Salle, of Duluth, of La Mothe Cadillac the founder of Detroit, Mackenzie, Fraser, Alexander Henry, and of the famous Scotch fur-kings, who governed the fate of the North-West. There is the greatest River in the world. Crossing it is a bridge that was long the engineering wonder of the world. There are the headquarters of the greatest railway in the world. Here is the strongest Bank on the continent. Nearer still is the wealthiest institution on the continent, the Seminary of St. Sulpice. In this tower is the largest bell on the continent." And so on.

The city's most pleasing source of interest, however, is its **historical spots** and associations, for in such there is scarcely a town in America richer, though, as in most active places, the march of progress has removed only. too many of the old houses, churches and streets. To what remain, we hope to conduct the reader. Among additional attractions of Montreal is McGill University, while the churches and charitable institutions and the athletic sports of the place are celebrated over the world.

The population at the end of French rule in 1760 was some 3,000; in 1809, about 12,000. To-day it is, as already stated, verging on 300,000? Its shipping trade, founded on the ancient annual barter between the Indian tribes here, amounted in 1840 to 31,266 tons burden, in 1891 to some 2,000,000 tons, nearly equally divided between ocean-going and inland vessels; while the number of its transatlantic steamship lines was 15, and the capital of its 11 banks $43,583,000.

**The Harbour.**—Prior to 1851 only vessels under 600 tons, and drawing not more than 11 feet of water, could pass up to Montreal; but, by degrees culminating lately, a channel 27½ feet deep has been dredged all the way up, so as to admit of the largest ships reaching the port from the Atlantic Ocean. At the same time, the inland canals have been deepened to 14 feet. Immense shipments of grain, lumber and cattle are exported by these means, and general imports return in exchange. Steam navigation was introduced early. In 1807 Fulton launched the first steamboat in America on the Hudson. Two years later, after correspondence with Fulton, an enterprising citizen launched here the first steamboat on the St. Lawrence. A tablet records his act as follows: "To the Honorable John Molson, the Father of Steam Navigation on the St. Lawrence. He launched the steamer 'Accommodation,' for Montreal and Quebec service, 1809."

At the upper end of the harbour enters the **Lachine Canal**, begun in 1821, after many delays and misgivings, yet at first but 5 feet deep and 48 wide at the waterline, and 28 at the bottom. Still, it was then wider and deeper than any similar work in England, and was considered a superior piece of masonry work.

**The Victoria Bridge,** crossing just above the harbour, was, when erected, "the greatest work of engineering skill in the world." The idea was the conception of a man foremost in advancing the trade of the town and its public works, the late Honorable John Young; and the work itself was designed by the celebrated English engineer, Robert Stephenson. It is erected in strong tubular form, resting on heavy stone abutments, calculated to stand the ice-crushes of spring, and was inaugurated publicly by the Prince of Wales in 1860. It "consists," says the inscription on a medal struck at the time, "of 23 spans 242 feet each, and one in centre 330 feet, with a long abutment on each bank of the River. The tubes are iron, 22 feet high, 16 feet wide, and weigh 6,000 tons, supported on 24 piers containing 250,000 tons of stone measuring 3,000,000 cubit feet. Extreme length, 2 miles; cost, $7,000,000." These figures and its massive construction show it to be many times more expensive and solid than present-day science

VICTORIA BRIDGE ON GRAND TRUNK RAILWAY.

would consider necessary for the purpose, and may be contrasted with the light cantilever bridge of the Canadian Pacific Railway at Lachine. It was built for the Grand Trunk Railway of Canada, of which it remains the property. Victoria Bridge is, in many respects, a study in itself, the nice allowance for expansion and contraction by temperature, the tons of paint applied to it, the half-ton of annual rust scraped off, and many other details, are food for curiosity and thought. All the iron came out from England, each piece marked for its place, the stone mostly from Pointe Claire. In an enclosure near the entrance to the bridge an immense boulder attracts curiosity. It bears an inscription stating that it was erected as a monument by the workmen engaged in building the bridge to the memory of 6,000 immigrants who died in one year of ship fever. The boulder was taken out of the bed of the River.

As the eye ranges about the harbour, it is caught by the long range of solid stone buildings which form the front of the city, by the great grain elevaters grouped at each end of the view, by the domes, towers and spires of the Bonsecours Market, Bonsecours Church, Notre Dame, the Custom House, and the Harbor Commissioners' Building, and the serried masts and the smokestacks of many iron steamships crowding the wharves. The landscape is one also full of history and tragedy.

---

(**The Canadian Pacific Railway Bridge** referred to, at Lachine, seven miles above, was completed in 1887. It is composed of 2 abutments and 15 piers. There are 4 land spans of 80 feet; the rest are 240 each, except the deep-water portion, consisting of 2 flanking spans of 270 feet and 2 cantilever, each 408, forming one continuous truss 1,356 feet long.)

Many a pre-historic savage fight must have taken place in the neighborhood : many a canoe of painted warriors have crept stealthily along the shores. On the shores round about, many a party of the settlers was murdered by the Iroquois in the earliest days of the colony. Two lost their lives in the same manner on St. Helen's Island just opposite; and on Moffatt's, or Isle-à-la-Pierre, Father Guillaume Vignal was slain by an Iroquois ambush during a fierce battle on the opening of a quarry in 1659. On the Longueuil bank opposite might, during the 18th century, have been descried the towers, walls and chapel spire of the finest feudal castle in New France. At St. Lambert there was a palisaded fort. Laprairie, far over to the south, across the water, was the scene, in 1691, of the celebrated and desperate battle of Laprairie, the first land attack by British colonists upon Canada. To the port came Indian traders for a generation before the founding of the city. Thither in succeeding days came down the processions of huge canoes of gaily-singing *voyageurs*, returning from a year's adventurous trading in the pathless regions of the West to the annual two months' fair at Montreal.

To speak of the Harbour is to speak of the River, which recalls a remark made in an antiquated description of Montreal. "A striking feature in this majestic stream," says *Hochelaga Depicta*, " independently of its magnitude, has always been the theme of just admiration. The Ottawa joins the St. Lawrence above, and thenceforward they unite their streams. But though they flow in company, each preserves its independence as low down as Three Rivers, ninety miles below

Montreal. . . . . . From any elevated part of the shore the spectator may discern the beautiful green tinge of the St. Lawrence on the farther side, and the purplish brown of the Ottawa on the half of the River nearest to him."

The city proper occupies only about 7,000 acres in area, being densely populated by reason of the climate. It is colloquially divided into "Uptown" and "Downtown," separated by an indefinite line about Dorchester Street. "East-end" and "West-end" are also terms frequently used, and the line is about Bleury Street. A convenient landmark is the intersection of the city by two principal business streets—St. Catherine, running across it from east to west, and St. Lawrence, from north to south.

The population is divided into three chief race divisions, coinciding also with religious lines: "English," inhabiting mainly the West-end, numbering about 60,000, and comprising a population much more decidedly Scottish than English in extraction; French, in number about 150,000, inhabiting principally the East-end, but also considerable portions of the lower levels of the West-end, as well as the adjoining cities of Ste. Cunegonde and St. Henri de Montreal; and "Irish," that is, Irish Roman Catholic, inhabiting the region known as "Griffintown," west of McGill Street, and numbering about 40,000.

The principal residential quarter is the "West-end," especially around and above Sherbrooke Street, which is the finest residence thoroughfare, though perhaps soon to be outdone by Pine and Cedar Avenues, on Mount Royal.

Architecturally, the city presents a solid appearance resembling that of the commercial British cities, the prevailing material being an admirable grey limestone, obtained from quarries in the neighborhood, relieved occasionally by stones of richer color, and for the cheaper buildings by a plain red brick.

The value of real estate in the town is approximately $150,000,000. The total annual revenue is $2,225,000, and is levied chiefly by an assessment of 1 per cent. on realty for civic purposes, 1-5 of 1 per cent. for schools, water rates, and business duty of 7½ per cent. on the rentals. Religious and benevolent institutions are exempt from taxation. The civic debt is over $16,000,000, and is limited to 15 per cent. of the assessed value of the real estate, a limit nearly reached. The debt is very largely represented, however, by valuable assets, such as Parks, City Hall, Fire Stations and Waterworks.

Having thus outlined the Montreal of to-day, a word remains about the Montreal of the future. No one can doubt that Nature intends a great city here. The head of ocean navigation on so matchless a waterway as the St. Lawrence—a seaport six hundred miles inland—with behind it the whole "north coast" of the United States, and such teeming cities as Chicago, Detroit, Buffalo, Toledo and Duluth, as well as the commerce of Canada, her growth must be great, steady and certain. History has always said so in the constant importance and steady advance of this point. The hopefulness, the pride of the Montrealer can only find full expression in verse:

CANADIAN PACIFIC RAILWAY BRIDGE.

Reign on, majestic Ville-Marie!
   Spread wide thy ample robes of state;
   The heralds cry that thou art great,
And proud are thy young sons of thee.
Mistress of half a continent,
   Thou risest from thy girlhood's rest;
   We see thee conscious heave thy breast
And feel thy rank and thy descent.
Sprung of the saint and chevalier,
   And with the Scarlet Tunic wed!
   Mount Royal's crown upon thy head,
And past thy footstool, broad and clear,
   St. Lawrence sweeping to the sea:
   Reign on, majestic Ville-Marie!

## CHAPTER III.

### SQUARES, PARKS AND CEMETERIES.

#### *I.—Squares.*

**Custom House Square,** a little space on the river front, is interesting on account of the early historical scenes associated with it, for it is the oldest square in Montreal. Most of its original extent is occupied by the Inland Revenue Building, or Old Custom House, a tablet upon which reads: "The first Public Square of Montreal, 1657—'La Place du Marché'—Granted by the Seigneurs, 1676." Here the French executions took place, of which one, described further on under "The Legend of the Croix Rouge," may be taken as an example. Facing the river one obtains, from the harbour ramp, a fine view of the large ocean shipping and maze of other craft which crowd the port, and look strange so far inland. To the right is seen the broad Foundling Street, the former bed of one of the two branches of the **Little River of Montreal,** which meandered from

Lachine, this branch running into the St. Lawrence here. It was covered over some two generations ago, but still flows underneath the street.

The **Custom House,** the handsome towered building of triangular form which stands upon the little cape once made by this stream with the St. Lawrence, is to the Montrealer something of what the Capitol was to Rome; for here Samuel de Champlain, that undaunted and patient Governor who founded Quebec and made French Canada, sojourned in 1611, when on the lookout for the site for a town, planted two gardens, built walls of clay, and, as we have previously narrated, called the spot **La Place Royale.** Traders with the Indians thenceforward made this convenient point their annual resort, until, in 1642, the town was founded.

## The Foundation of Montreal.

The story in brief is as follows: Jean Jacques Olier, a dainty courtier abbé of Paris, having become religiously awakened, renounced his worldly enjoyments and vanities, and threw himself with fervor into new movements of Catholic piety originated by himself. He distinguished himself, to the great disgust of his aristocratic friends, by an unwonted care of the popular wants as *curé* of the large Parish of St. Sulpice in Paris. He then took up the work of organizing the education of young priests, and established to that end, as the first of many such, the Seminary of St. Sulpice at Paris. Accounts of the heathen tribes about the Island of Montreal having reached him, his fervent meditations conceived the project of founding a mission in that region; and when travelling, about this time, he met one de la Dauversière, a receiver of taxes in Brittany, who, it appeared, had been taken up with much the same idea. Divine miracle, it was believed, lit the project simultaneously in their breasts and brought the two together, for though they were strangers, they seemed immediately to recognize each other, and rushed into an embrace. "It was at Meudon," says a modern French writer, "at the door of the Palace, whither the Sieur de la Dauversière had come to request the aid of the Minister for his enterprise. The two men, *who had never before seen each other, illumined suddenly by a light within*, fall into each other's arms, call each other by name, treat each other like brothers, relate their mutual plans, speak at length of this colony of Montreal (which was still but an unknown island), with topographical details so exact that one would have said they had passed long years together there."

They obtained the aid of a number of wealthy and noble persons of the court, including the Duchesse de Bullion, and these were formed into a society known as the Company of Our Lady of Montreal (Compagnie de Notre Dame de Montréal).

About the same time a young nun of great devotion and much given to ecstasies and visions, Mademoiselle Jeanne Mance by name, believed herself called in a vision to go to the same place, and there to found a convent and mission. To her, too, the miraculous is ascribed. "God lifting for her the veils of space, showed to her, while yet in France, *in a divine vision, the shores of our isle, and the site of Ville Marie at the foot of its*

*Mountain and on the shore of its great River."* "Why," says a later writer, " should we refuse to believe this tale?"

Combining crusader and martyr spirits, they purposely chose the most dangerous outpost, and to that end acquired the Island of Montreal, then uninhabited, distant and exposed to the incursions of the powerful Iroquois. Paul de Chomédy, Sieur de Maisonneuve, a gentleman of Champagne, and a brave and ascetic knight of the mediæval school, was entrusted with the command. He landed, with the Governor, De Montmagny, Father Vimont a Jesuit, Mlle. Mance, another woman and fifty-five male colonists, on the 18th of May, 1642, a momentous day for Montreal. Tents were pitched, camp fires lighted, evening fell, and mass was held. Fire-flies, caught and imprisoned in a phial upon the altar, served as lights, and the little band were solemnly addressed by Vimont in words which included these: " You are a grain of mustard seed that shall rise and grow till its branches overshadow the earth. You are few, but your work is the work of God. His smile is upon you, and your children shall fill the land." Two tablets on the front of the Custom House record the above facts as follows: " This Site was selected and named in 1611 La Place Royale, by Samuel de Champlain, the Founder of Canada;" and, " Near this spot, on the 18th day of May, 1642, landed the Founders of Montreal, commanded by Paul de Chomédy, Sieur de Maisonneuve: Their first proceeding was a religious service."

The new settlement was named Ville Marie, in honor

of the patron saint of the fraternity, "The Queen of Heaven." As they held that the Island was peopled by demons, they sang the *Te Deum* very loudly and defiantly and fired cannon to drive them away, and had the good fortune to do so.

A picket fort was commenced and mounted with cannon, and this enclosure, known sometimes as the **Fort de Ville-Marie,** stood on Commissioners' Street, just behind the thoroughfare in rear of the Custom House, known as Port Street, where another tablet records its site thus: "Here was the Fort of Ville-Marie, first dwelling-place of the Founders of Ville-Marie, built 1643, demolished 1648. Replaced by the House of Monsieur de Callières, 1686."

For nearly a quarter of a century the inhabitants could not leave its limits without danger of an attack from the Iroquois foes, with whom the French were at war. The Legendary Dog of Ville-Marie, **Pilote** by name, was accustomed to take her daily rounds among the woods in this neighborhood, with her litter of pups, hunting about for lurking Iroquois. Many a spot in the present city can be pointed out as the scene of the death of some member of the little community, and every acre in this neighborhood has been covered by hostile footsteps. The spirit of chivalry which was dying out in Europe was transplanted hither, and has made the early history of Montreal a tale of romance and danger approached by that of no other new-world town.

Near by, on Foundling Street, is a tablet marking the site of the **Residence of Governor de Callières,** which replaced the Fort de Ville-Marie: "Site of the Chateau of Louis Hector de Callières, Governor of Montreal 1684, of New France 1698-1703. He terminated the fourteen years' war with the Iroquois by treaty at Montreal, 1701." Callières was the staunchest Governor New France ever had except Frontenac. Charlevoix declares him to have been even better as a general.

Behind the square, somewhat later, stood the first Manor House, for the Island had its feudal lords. These were the **Gentlemen of the Seminary of St. Sulpice,** as they are still called, who yet retain a faint semblance of the position. The site of the first Manor House is in the small court of Frothingham & Workman, reached by an open passage from St. Paul Street. The tablet upon the present warehouse reads as follows: "Upon this foundation stood the first Manor House of Montreal, built 1661, burnt 1852, re-built 1853. It was the Seminary of St. Sulpice from 1661 to 1712. Residence of de Maisonneuve, Governor of Montreal, and of Pierre Raimbault, Civil and Criminal Lieutenant-General."

Under the régime of the latter it was also the prison.

A block deeper within the city than Custom House Square is

**The Place d'Armes**—The centre of the city's life. At no other spot do so many interests—English, French, business, historical, religious—meet. In the centre stands\* the statue of Maisonneuve. It is of bronze, and represents him in the cuirass and French costume

---

\* Or, rather (February, 1892), is to stand.

of the 17th century, holding the fleur-de-lys banner. The pedestal, of granite, shows the inscription : " Paul de Chomedy de Maisonneuve, Foundateur de Montréal, 1642." It rests upon a fountain, and displays several bas-reliefs, representing respectively : (1), Maisonneuve killing the Indian Chief; (2), the founding of Ville-Marie ; (3), the death of Lambert Closse, Town Major of the devoted band, who had hoped for a death fighting the Heathen, and who, in fact, so died, defending his own enclosure near St. Lambert Hill ; (4), the still more heroic death of Dollard, who fell with his companions at the Long Sault of the Ottawa, and so saved the colony. At the four corners of the base are four life-size bronze figures, representing respectively an Indian, a colonist's wife, a colonist, with the legendary dog Pilote, and a soldier.

Facing the square from Notre Dame Street stand the tall and stiff façade and towers of the Parish Church, **Nôtre Dame de Montréal,** a building not beautiful, but which all admit to be impressive. The style is a composite Gothic, an adaptation of different varieties to one severe design, of a French trend, though the architect was a Protestant named O'Donnell. He afterwards became a Roman Catholic, and is buried in the vaults beneath. The interior, from its breadth, its ampleness, its rich decorations, and the powerful appearance of its two great tiers of galleries, is still more impressive than the front. The wealth of the adjoining Seminary, its proprietors, has been freely spent upon it, as well as the revenues of a vast congregation, and, holding as it sometimes does at great celebrations, not far from 15,000 people, it is the chief temple of a whole race. Among the objects to be noticed are: The Baptistery, to the right on entering, especially its exquisite stained glass windows; the small altar-picture of the black Virgin, the original of which is attributed by legend to the brush of St. Luke, and is claimed to be miracle-working; the beautiful wood-carving under it of the Entombment of Christ; a small marble statue, given by Pope Pius IX., on the pillar near the Grand Altar, and for praying before which the inscription promises an indulgence of 100 days from purgatory; the bronze St. Peter at the opposite pillar, whose foot is kissed by the faithful in the same manner as the original statue in St. Peter's at Rome; and others in great variety. The Grand Altar proper is a fine piece of work from the artistic point of view, and the white carved groups upon it, representing the Redeemer's sacrifice in various forms, are notable. They are by a modern German master. Some Venetian figures at the sides, above the choir, are, however, in very bad taste. Above this altar one may catch a glimpse, through the opening, of the richly-carved new Gothic Lady-Chapel in rear, which is reached by passing through the doors near at hand, and though somewhat overgilt, well merits inspection. The organ, a new one, built by the Brothers Casavant, of St. Hyacinthe, is claimed to be the finest on the continent, and the splendid orchestra and choir make it a rare musical treat to attend one of the great festival services, Christmas, Epiphany, Easter and others. The towers are 227 feet high. The ascent part-way is made by means of an elevator in the west tower, as far up as the great bell,

"Le Gros Bourdon," which is only sounded on the most solemn occasions, such as the death of a Pope, and is the largest bell in America. Its weight is 24,780 pounds. Ten other large bells are found in the opposite tower; 18 men are required to ring them. Ascending further, to the top of the west tower, the finest obtainable view of the harbor and lower town is had.

The earliest church of Montreal was one of bark, built in the original Fort. This was replaced in 1656 by the first Parish Church, on the north corner of the present St. Sulpice and St. Paul Streets, where a tablet marks its site thus: "Here was the first Parish Church of Ville-Marie, erected in 1656." In 1672 the latter was in its turn replaced by what is now known as the Old Parish Church, which stood across Notre Dame Street. Its picturesque belfry tower remained alone on the corner of the square for some years after the removal of the old church, but was taken down about 1840. The foundations yet exist under the south gate of the square. The cut-stone front, designed by King's Engineer, De Léry, the same who erected the stone fortification walls of the city, and who also designed the Cathedral of Quebec, was, when taken down, used as a front for the Recollets Church, and after the demolition of the latter, was incorporated in the back walls of the store upon its site, where some of the pieces are still to be seen. The furniture and pictures were sent to the Church of Bonsecours, and the pulpit chair of the Unitarian Church is made out of timbers of the tower. A tablet on the adjoining wall of the Seminary reads: "The second Parish Church of Ville-Marie, built in

1672, dedicated 1678, and demolished in 1829, occupied the middle of Notre Dame Street."

A whimsical "legend" has long been told of the corner of the present Church, on St. Sulpice Street, where there is always a little breeze, even in the hottest weather.

The Devil and the Wind, runs the story, were walking down Notre Dame Street, when this Church had just been built. "Why," said the Devil, "what is this? I never saw this before." "I dare you to go in," replied the Wind. "You dare me, do you? You wait here till I come out," cried the Devil. "I'll be at the corner," said the Wind. His Majesty went in. He has never yet come out, and the Wind has remained ever since waiting for him at the corner.

The quaint, black-faced **Seminary of St. Sulpice,** erected in 1710, adjoins the Parish Church. Its revenues are immense, but the amount is never made public. The Seminary at Paris, of which this is a branch, obtained the Island from De Maisonneuve's Association in 1663 under charge of keeping up church services and providing for education. The building contains the baptismal and other registers of the city from the beginning, besides uncounted wealth of other historical treasures. The old fleur-de-lys still caps its pinnacles, old French roof-curves cover the walls, and as the priests nearly all come from France, there is a complete old-world flavor about the institution. In the words of Charlevoix, it was "a stately, great and pleasant House, built of Free-stone, after the model of that of St. Sulpice at Paris; and the Altar stands by itself, just like that at Paris."

The tablets here read: " The Seminary of St. Sulpice, founded at Paris, by Monsieur Jean Jacques Olier, 1641; established at Ville-Marie, 1657, Monsieur Gabriel de Queylus, Superior. Seigneurs of the Island of Montreal, 1663." And: " François Dollier de Casson, First Historian of Montreal, Captain under Marshal de Turenne, then Priest of St. Sulpice during 35 years. He died, in 1701, curé of the Parish."

SEMINARY OF ST. SULPICE.

The latter tablet refers to a most attractive, pleasant and somewhat whimsical narrator—Dollier de Casson—on whose *Histoire du Montréal* all the completer historians largely draw.

Opposite Notre Dame are the Bank of Montreal and the Imperial Insurance Building. To the north, the tall red stone building is that of the New York Life Insurance Company, from the tower of which a good view may be obtained. On the south corner, the prominent edifice is that of the Royal Insurance Company. On the east corner is one of the Antiquarian Society's tablets, on the site of a dwelling of the famous Du Luth, reading as follows: "Here lived, in 1675, Daniel de Grésolon, Sieur Dulhut, one of the explorers of the Upper Mississippi; after whom the City of Duluth was named."

The face of the **Imperial Building** shows two tablets, one of which reads: "Near this Square, afterwards named La Place d'Armes, the founders of Ville-Marie first encountered the Iroquois, whom they defeated, Chomédy de Maisonneuve killing the Chief with his own hands, 30 March, 1644."

The story is that one winter, de Maisonneuve, being besieged in the fort by his savage foes, kept his people shut up out of harm's way. Some of them charged him with cowardice, and insisted on being led forth. Finally he acceded. The woods hereabout suddenly swarmed with yelling savages, and the French, to avoid a massacre, broke for the fort. Maisonneuve was the last to withdraw, and, as he did so, he fought hand-to-hand with a gigantic chief, who hurled himself upon the commander, eager for distinction as the bravest "brave." Maisonneuve withstood and slew him in single combat, and then retired slowly to the fort. Thenceforward those who had maligned him were silenced. It is disputed whether this neighborhood or Custom House Square was the approximate scene of the conflict; but the distance between the two is not great, in the direct line.

The other inscription records the interesting fact that

the Imperial Building stands upon the second lot granted on the Island of Montreal. The first was another on the same square—the property adjoining the Royal Insurance Company's—which still belongs to a male lineal descendant of the original grantee, Father Toupin of St. Patrick's Church.

On this square the French, American and British armies have successively paraded as possessors of the town, and here the French army solemnly surrendered its arms, in the presence of the troops of Amherst, in 1760.

**The Bank of Montreal,** with a capital and rest of $18,000,000, is said to be the strongest financial institution in America. Its fine Corinthian structure, noted for its classical purity of line, looks like the spirit of ancient Greece among the modern edifices by which it is surrounded. Originally it possessed a dome. The counting-room is fitted and frescoed with scenes from Canadian history, such as to repay examination. The Bank was organized in 1817, and is the oldest bank in Canada. The sculpture on the pediment in front is the work of John Steel, R.S.A., her Majesty's sculptor in Scotland. The arms of the Bank, with the motto "Concordia Salus," forms the centre of the group. On each side is an Indian, one barbaric, the other becoming civilized. The other two figures are a settler and a sailor, the former with a pipe of peace in his hand, reclining upon logs and surrounded by the implements of industry and culture. The sailor is pulling at a rope, and is appropriately surrounded with the emblems of commerce. Upon the building a tablet reads: "The

Stone Fortifications of Ville-Marie extended from Dalhousie Square through this site to McGill Street, thence south to Commissioners Street, and along the latter to the before-mentioned Square. Begun 1721 by Chaussegros de Léry. Demolished 1817."

Next to the Bank of Montreal is the **Post Office,** a handsome building in the Renaissance style, now too small for the volume of business.

Opposite it is some of the Seminary's real estate—a striking illustration of the non-progressiveness of old tenures.

Passing westward along St. James Street, we come to **Victoria Square,** situated at the foot of Beaver Hall Hill, and intersected by Craig Street. Leading mercantile houses surround it. It receives its name from the beautiful bronze statue of Queen Victoria, by the English sculptor, Marshall Wood. Looking upwards from the foot of the square, one sees a bit of Mount Royal in the distance, while nearer by are a range of church spires, being respectively, counting from left to right, St. Andrew's Presbyterian, the Reformed Episcopal, Christ Church Cathedral, the Church of the Messiah (facing from Beaver Hall Hill), and St. Patrick's. This square was the old-time Haymarket. It is a busy neighborhood, on the edge of the heart of the town, and is crossed at morning and evening by the principal business people who reach the West-End by Beaver Hall Hill. On the Unitarian Church on the hill a tablet runs: "Here stood Beaver Hall, built 1800, burnt 1848; Mansion of Joseph Frobisher, one of the founders of The North-West Company, which made Montreal for years the fur-trading centre of America." This building, celebrated only as a landmark, was a long wooden cottage facing down the slope, and was partly protected in front by tall poplar trees. It was the nearest to town of the pleasant suburban seats of the Old North-Westers which covered the slopes of Mount Royal.

**Fortification Lane** commences at this square, and marks the line of the old French fortifications. They were of stone, in bastioned form, running along the course of this lane, to its end, then across the Champ de Mars, and eastward, to include Dalhousie Square, by the Quebec Gate Station. Thence they returned along the water front to the present McGill Street, which was their westerly limit. The exits were few, being the Récollet Gate at this end and the Quebec at the other, with the St. Lawrence Gate on the land side and several openings on the river, called the Small, the Market, the St. Mary's and the Water Gate. Craig Street was then a suburban swamp, with a branch of the Little River running through.

Near by, at the corner of Notre Dame Street, is a tablet thus marking the site of the memorable Récollet Gate: "Récollets Gate: By this gate Amherst took possession, 8th September, 1760. General Hull, U.S. Army, 25 officers, 350 men, entered prisoners of war, 20 September, 1812." General Amherst, the British commander, after the capitulation by the French Governor, de Vaudreuil, ordered Colonel Frederick Haldimand to receive the keys of the city and occupy the western quarter of it. That officer at once did so with his brigade, and was the first Englishman to pass the walls

VICTORIA SQUARE.

of the new possession. Nothing now remains of the old fortifications except their foundations buried in the soil. They were built, in 1723, by the king's engineer, Chaussegros de Léry, and replaced a smaller wall of palisades, erected about 1685 by command of Governor de Callières, to protect against the Iroquois.

Proceeding eastward along Craig Street, past some nine cross-streets, we come to

**Viger Square,** extending for several blocks on Craig Street East, at the corner of St. Denis Street. It receives its name from Commander Jacques Viger, the first Mayor of Montreal, a man of spirit, and the father of local antiquarianism. With its well-grown trees, its ponds and greenhouse, it is the pride of the principal French residence quarter. Large crowds attend in the evenings to listen to the music of favorite bands, which is of a high order, the French-Canadians making excellent musicians.

In sight of Viger Square, westward, on the hillside, is the long

**Champ de Mars,** the military parade-ground of the British garrisons when they existed here. It is a level piece of ground surrounded by decayed poplar trees, and overlooked by the Court House, City Hall, St. Gabriel Church (the first Protestant Church erected in the city) and the Provincial Government Building, formerly the residence of the Hon. Peter McGill, first English Mayor of Montreal, 1840. The Champ was originally—that is to say, during French times, before 1760—very much smaller, being only the space enclosed by the 3rd Bastion of the city walls; but it was enlarged, in the early years of the century, by means of the earth obtained from removing Citadel Hill. The foundation of the walls runs underneath the surface along the middle of the square, and has been exposed to view in excavations. This was a gay neighborhood during the palmy days of the garrison, when some of the most famous regiments of the British army, such as the Guards, were stationed here.

Adjoining the Champ de Mars, and passing between the Court House and City Hall, towards the harbour, is **Jacques Cartier Square,** the upper part of which was, in early times, the **Place des Jesuites,** for the east end of the Court House borders the site of the French Jesuits' Monastery, used afterwards as military quarters, and later replaced by the Gaol and the former Court House, which in turn were replaced, about 1856, by the present "Palace of Justice." In the Monastery of the Jesuits lodged the celebrated historian Charlevoix, to whom a tablet erected there runs: "The Père Charlevoix, historian of La Nouvelle France, 1725." The foundations can be traced on the square.

Another tablet on the same building reflects a vivid picture of early times: the torturing by fire, on the square, of four Iroquois prisoners, who thus suffered death, by a stern order of Governor Count Frontenac in 1696, in reprisal for the torturing of French prisoners taken by their tribes. The expedient was successful. The whole inscription is: "Here stood the Church, Chapel and Residence of the Jesuit Fathers. Built 1692, occupied as military headquarters 1800. Burnt 1803. Charlevoix and Lafitau, among others, sojourned here. On the square in front, four Iroquois suffered death by fire, in reprisal, by order of Frontenac, 1696." The same spot was, in later days—even within the memory of men now living—the place where stood the Town Pillory, an antiquated institution which seems almost incredible to our present-day imaginations.

A tablet on the City Hall, just opposite, connects the square with its protonym thus : " To Jacques Cartier, celebrated navigator of St. Malo. Discovered Canada, and named the St. Lawrence, 1534–1535."

The part of the square between Notre Dame Street and the harbour is in the midst of the oldest neighbourhood of buildings in Montreal, some of the little streets (such as St. Amable Street) being, in their entirety, not less than a century old, and completely in the antique spirit. A glance around from Notre Dame Street will make this evident.

To the east, on the corner, is the old **Store of the Compagnie des Indes,** which, in the French times, answered to the Hudson Bay Company. It bears also a tablet that speaks for itself: " The Residence of the Honourable James McGill, Founder of McGill University, 1744–1813." The heavy stone vaulting of the cellars is worth a glance within.

Just beyond it, in a garden, is the **Château de Ramezay** (1705) the residence of one of the French and some of the British Governors—a good old family mansion of the time when this was the aristocratic end of the city.

In front, at the end of the square, is **Nelson's Column,** surmounted by a statue of the one-armed hero, Lord Nelson himself, strangely enough, with his back to the water! It was erected, in 1809, by subscription among both English and French residents. The inscriptions may be read for completer information.

The rest of the square is a public open market, used every Tuesday and Friday. On its lower part, near St. Paul Street, is the site of the old Château de Vaudreuil, the residence of the last French Governor of Canada, who retired to France, with the army of his country, after surrendering the city and province to General

CHÂTEAU DE RAMEZAY.

Amherst in 1760. The château was a miniature court of France. The present square, its garden, saw the presence of Montcalm, Beaujeu, Levis and many another brave soldier of the old time, as well as those brilliant embezzlers and voluptuaries, Bigot, Cadet, Varin and the rest. The same site was previously that of the large residence of the famous Du Luth. A tablet just above

St. Paul Street reads: "The Château de Vaudreuil was built opposite, in 1723, by the Marquis de Vaudreuil, Governor-General; residence of the Marquis de Vaudreuil-Cavagnal, his son, the last Governor of New France. Montcalm, Lévis, Bourlamaque, Bougainville, sojourned here."

A short distance eastward is

**Dalhousie Square,** the site of the ancient French citadel, having been a steep eminence until its levelling, in 1819, by permission of the Governor, Earl Dalhousie. It formerly bore the name of Citadel Hill. The "Citadel" was a wooden blockhouse, which commanded the principal streets from end to end, and its situation, the summit of the rising, was afterwards for a time occupied by the second rude waterworks of Montreal. The town walls ended here with the **Quebec Gate,** a name which still clings to the locality. The district beyond is popularly known as "the Quebec Suburbs." Adjoining is the East-end, or Quebec Gate, Station of the Canadian Pacific Railway, built upon the site of the old French Arsenal, later used as Barracks by the British garrison. At its demolition, a few years ago, to make way for the station, the last part of the French fortification walls of the city was removed. The following tablet is proposed for the Railway Station: "This Square occupies the site of La Citadelle, built in 1685, replacing the mill erected by Maisonneuve and Dailleboust in 1660. Royal Battery 1723. Levelled and presented to the city by Earl Dalhousie, Governor-General, 1821. Near the east corner of Nôtre Dame Street stood the Porte St. Martin (Quebec Gate).

Ethan Allen entered it prisoner of war, 1775. This station replaced the French Arsenal, removed 1881, with the last portion of the fortification walls of 1721." The hill itself was a curious piece of alluvial formation, the culmination of that long ridge formed by the branching of the Little River of Montreal into two, on which the French city of Montreal was built, the waters in a former age having apparently washed the soil into this shape. A similar mound and ridge, exhibiting perfectly the

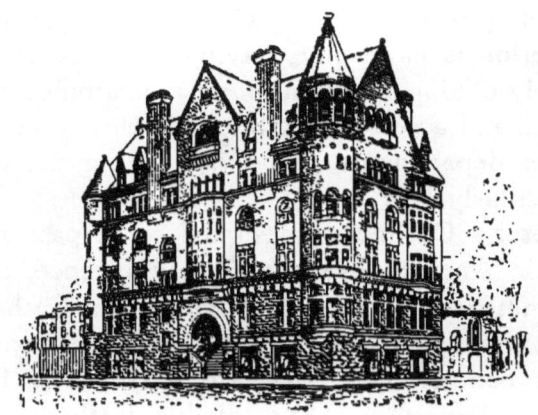

Y.M.C.A. BUILDING, DOMINION SQUARE.

manner of its formation, exists at the mouth of the River Châteauguay some fifteen miles distant.

Leaving "down-town," and striking westward much farther, we come to

**Dominion Square,** which represents the westward-moving growth and life of Montreal. Situated in the best neighbourhood of the city, it is a plain, open square with turf and beds of flowers, and is cut into two by Dorchester Street West, at which part are placed two

Russian cannon taken in the Crimean war. Around, in order, are : the Windsor Hotel, Dominion Square Methodist Church and parsonage, St. George's Anglican Church, parsonage and school, the headquarters and West-end Station of the Canadian Pacific Railway, the Roman Catholic Archbishop's Palace and his Cathedral of St. Peter's, and the **Young Men's Christian Association.** The latter is a large and beautiful seven-story building of rich-colored pressed brick, with ample facings of grey cut stone. The style is Queen Anne. The interior is handsome, having a first-class hall, a completely-equipped gymnasium, a magnificent swimming-bath and accessories, a bright reading-room, library and other departments. The views from the windows are particularly fine.

**St. Peter's Cathedral,** designed to surpass all other temples in America in size and magnificence, is a copy of the immense St. Peter's of Rome, the Cathedral of all Catholicism, of which it is half the dimensions. The idea was conceived by the late Archbishop Bourget, after the burning, in 1854, of his Cathedral of St. Jacques, then on St. Denis Street. The architect was Victor Bourgeau, who went to Rome to study the original. The foundations were commenced in 1870. Even after it commenced the enterprise seemed for a number of years to threaten failure on account of the expense ; but by assessing every head in the large diocese, this was ultimately met. The Cathedral is built in the form of a cross, 330 feet long and 222 wide. The masonry works of the great dome are 138 feet in height above the floor. The chief respects, besides size, in which the design differs from St. Peter's of Rome, are that the roof is inclined, on account of our snowfall, and the sides are both similar, whereas one side of the Roman Cathedral is elaborately columned in cut stone. The differences may be examined on a model in wood which is exhibited in the interior. The stone-work of the façade is the handsomest portion of the Cathedral, the carving of the immense blocks used for the capitals of columns being very fine. To obtain perfect stones large enough for these pieces occasioned many months of delay in the erection of the portico. The dome is by most people considered the great feature, and dominates all parts of the city. It is 70 feet in diameter at its commencement, and its summit is 210 feet from the spectators on floor of the Church. It is an exact copy of the famous dome of St. Peter's, Rome, the work of Brunelleschi, and is 250 feet in height to the top of the cross—46 feet higher than the towers of Notre Dame. Above is a huge gilt ball, on which is placed a glittering cross, 18 feet high and 12 long. Four smaller domes surround the main one. The interior of the Church is not completed, but is interesting from its size and plan.

Close by is the Palace of the Roman Catholic Archbishop of Montreal, a plain brick building with chapel. The present Archbishop is Monseigneur Fabre.

**The Windsor Hotel** is the best in Canada, and one of the best-situated anywhere. Its dining-room and grand corridor are scarcely to be excelled in effect. It accommodates 700 guests.

**Windsor Hall**, adjoining it, is the largest hall in Canada, and is used for concerts.

**St. George's Church** is the place of worship of the second largest Anglican body. It is an example of the Decorated Gothic style, and possesses a number of excellent stained glass windows and a good carved front porch. The old flags of the Montreal Light Infantry (1837) are hung within. The service is Low Church.

WINDSOR HOTEL AND DOMINION SQUARE.

The square next worthy of notice is

**St. Louis Square,** the prettiest in Montreal, on Upper St. Denis Street, above Sherbrooke. It is small, but is embellished by a large rectangular pond, occupying its centre, the bright flat mass of which, with a distant view of Mount Royal visible, good trees around, and handsomely turreted houses of cut stone lining the surrounding streets, give it much beauty. It is constructed out of the former public "Tank" or water reservoir, discarded many years since. Numbers of the principal French people live in the vicinity, upon Sherbrooke, St. Denis and other streets.

**Phillips' Square,** above Beaver Hall Hill, on St. Catherine Street, is a small space grown with large trees. Christ Church Cathedral, Morgan's Store and the Art Gallery, all at the head of it on St. Catherine Street, are principal landmarks of the city.

A number of less notable squares might be enumerated if that were useful; but we pass on to the

## II.—*Parks.*

Montreal has three.

**Logan Park** is not yet finished, and may be left out of count. Of the other two—**Mount Royal** and **St. Helen's Island**—it may be doubted if any city in the world can produce a pair their equal in natural beauty.

**Mount Royal** is an ideal crown for a city. Not too lofty to be inaccessible, nor so low as to be insignificant, it presents, here bold rock-faces, there gentle green slopes, vistaed dales, clothed with great plenty of trees, ferns and wild flowers; meditative nooks, drives, wide prospects and look-outs. The long curve of its crest rises above the city in a perpetual invitation of sylvan charm and rest. The skirts of its slope, below the limits appropriated to the public park, are covered with *palazzi* and villas peeping out of the foliage. The park is approached usually from the south-east and north-east sides, in each case by a series of winding drives intersected by more direct footpaths. On the latter side (by Fletcher's Field), the " Mountain Elevator " carries passengers in four specially-constructed cars some distance up towards the foot of the chief ascent, and then climbs a precipitous steep to the crest. The charms of the mountain, however, are most thoroughly seen by following the course of the drives which encircle it, which were designed, together with the general plan of development of the Park, by the celebrated Frederick Law Olmsted, who laid out Central Park, New York. He has published a little book on Mount Royal, conveying his ideas for the future development of its beauties on natural principles. Among the landmarks most to be noticed are: the High Level Reservoir, the General City Reservoir (seen some distance below), the residence and grounds of the late Sir Hugh Allan, founder of the Allan Steamship Line, which, surrounded by a stone wall, is situated just adjoining the High Level Reservoir; the monumental pillar in the same place, over the grave of Simon McTavish, who, at the beginning of the century, was the chief partner in the North-West Company, which founded the modern commercial greatness of Montreal. Tradition has it (erroneously) that he committed suicide, and that his mansion, which long stood deserted a short distance below on the hillside, was haunted by spirits. A walk along the drive northward, skirting the precipitous face of the mountain, gives one of the most picturesque parts. At the western end of the drive, in this direction, one can push on by footpath through the forest and pass into the beautiful vale devoted to Mount Royal Cemetery. Returning to the High Level Reservoir, he has the choice of climbing by graduated flights of steps up the face of the cliff, and thus reaching the summit. Fine landscape views are obtained from all these points, especially from the top.

> Changing its hue with the changing skies,
>   The River flows in its beauty rare ;
> While across the plain eternal, rise
>   Boucherville, Rougemont and St. Hilaire.
> Far to the Westward lies Lachine,
>   Gate of the Orient long ago,
> When the virgin forest swept between
>   The Royal Mount and the River below.

The best points of view are Prospect Point, near the steps, the Look-out farther south (at which carriages stop), and the Observatory farther inwards. From these the city is seen in a rich panorama below. Past it flows the River, with its Island of St. Helen's, St. Paul's or Nun's Island, half in forest, half meadow, the French parish spires glittering here and there along its banks, and the Lachine Rapids gleaming in the distance. Beyond the River, the great plain of the Saint Lawrence Valley, broken by solitary, abrupt, single mountains here and there, and faintly hemmed in in the distance by the cloudlike outlines of the Green and Adirondack ranges. The solitary mountains referred to are of volcanic origin and are respectively, from east to west, Montarville, St. Bruno, Belœil (which stands out strong and abrupt), Rougemont, Yamaska and Mount Johnson. This volcanic sisterhood has a member in Mount Royal herself, for the latter is also an extinct volcano, and, in misty ages past, belched out lava over the prehistoric plain. The crater may still be seen on the principal crest, and the cone on the south side, not far off, while the rocks of the

LACHINE RAPIDS.

summit are of black lava crystals, as may be seen by examining them. The mountain was at that time a high one, with its base extending beyond St. Helen's Isle. There is a prophecy that some day the volcano will again open, and the city and island sink beneath the St. Lawrence. From the Observatory the view is enlarged by the half of the landscape looking across the back and upper and lower ends of the island. The quiet of the trim farms forms a striking contrast to the life of the city. The Rivière des Prairies, or Back River—a part of the Ottawa—is seen behind the island, at the head of which lies the bright surface of the Lake of Two Mountains. Far away, hemming in the horizon on that side, runs the hoary Laurentian range, the oldest hills known to geology. They are the boundaries of the unknown wilds of the North.

The mountain is about 900 feet above the level of the sea, and about 740 above the river-level. The park consists of 462 acres. It was acquired, in 1860, from various private proprietors, as a result of popular outcry over one of their number stripping his share of it of the timber, and thereby conspicuously disfiguring the side.

A tablet on the summit records the visit of Jacques Cartier to it in 1535.

The early records say that de Maisonneuve made a pilgrimage to the top, bearing a large cross on his shoulders, in the January of 1643, in fulfilment of a vow made in the winter on the occasion of a great flooding of the river, which swept up to the foot of the town palisades, and was, he believed, stayed by prayers. "The Jesuit Du Peron led the way, followed in procession by Madame de la Peltrie, the artisans and soldiers, to the destined spot. The commandant, who, with all the ceremonies of the Church, had been declared First Soldier of the Cross, walked behind the rest, bearing on his shoulders a cross so heavy that it needed his utmost strength to climb the steep and rugged path. They planted it on the highest crest, and all knelt in adoration before it. . . . . Sundry relics of saints had been set in the wood of the cross, which remained an object of pilgrimage to the pious colonists of Ville-Marie." *

A hundred years ago, all along the slopes below, towards the city, were perched the country seats of the old North-Westers, McTavish, McGillivray, Sir Alexander MacKenzie, the Frobishers, Clarke and others, most pleasant rural villas, abundant in all the hospitalities of olden time.

The mountain has been the occasional theme of numerous versifiers, but it has its poet in Mr. Walter

---

* Parkman : "The Jesuit in North America," pp. 263-4.

Norton Evans, to whom it was his delight and comfort during a period of recovery from loss of sight. In his volume, "Mount Royal," he says, with deep feeling:

> " O, Royal Mountain ! Holy Mount to me,
> I come to thee, as in bright days of yore :
> That by thy pure and calming ministry,
> In reverence and deep humility,
> I may be brought nearer the heart of God,
> And hear His voice in Nature's voice around."

Further on he describes the usual winter revels in certain localities :

> " Here, as I lie beneath the maple shade,
> How glorious a view is spread for me.
> There are "The Pines," where many a wild halloo
> On moonlight nights in winter, has aroused
> The sleeping echoes ; when the snowshoers,
> In blanket suit, with brightly-colored sash,
> And tuque of red or blue ; their mocassins
> Of moose-skin, smoothly drawn on well-socked foot,
> And snowshoe firmly bound with deer-skin thong—
> Wound up the hill in long extended files,
> Singing and shouting with impetuous glee.
>         \*    \*    \*    \*    \*
> While yonder lie the hill and meadow-land,
> Now emerald green, but on bright winter nights,
> Upon whose snowy bosom happy crowds
> Fly on the swift toboggan down the hill,
> And o'er the broad expanse."

At the close he again reverently apostrophises :

> " Mounts of Transfiguration still there are,
> That lift us far above the influence
> Of time and sense, and bring us nearer heaven :
> And such thou art to me.—When in the valley
> We feel our limitations, grieve and fret ;
> And then, in wild despair, look to the hills,
> For there are wisdom, strength and boundless love :
> Thou blessed mountain-teacher, Fare-thee-well ! "

**St. Helen's Island,** named affectionately by Champlain after his young wife, Hélène Boullé, lies like a gem in the wide St. Lawrence. The shades of its deep groves, standing opposite the city, seem to constantly beckon the heated citizen in summer. A considerable portion of it is reserved for military purposes, and a fort exists within the enclosure. In the days of British garrisons this was a gay place. It is now the resort, on hot days, of the crowded masses, to whom its shades and breezes are an inestimable boon. For their use it is provided with merry-go-rounds, refreshment-houses, games, an open swimming-bath at the lower end, and pleasant paths. The island was remarked upon by Champlain, on his 1611 visit, as a site for a strong town. He so greatly fancied it, that he purchased it, a little later, with money out of his wife's dowry. The registers of Notre Dame record that, on the 19th of August, 1664, two young men, Pierre Magnan and Jacques Dufresne, were slain here by Iroquois.

It seems to have been sometimes used by the French as a military station, for in June, 1687, the Chevalier de Vaudreuil posted both the regular troops and the militia there in readiness to march againt the Iroquois. Thither the Marquis de Lévis, commanding the last French army, withdrew, and here burnt his flags in the presence of his army the night previous to surrendering the colony to the English. Louis Honoré Frechette, the national French-Canadian poet, bases upon this his poem, entitled "All Lost but Honour."

In 1688 the island was acquired by Charles Le Moyne, Sieur de Longueuil, who gave the name of Ste. Hélène

MONTREAL FROM MOUNT ROYAL PARK.

to one of his most distinguished sons. During the eighteenth century (from before 1723), his descendants, the Barons of Longueuil, whose territory lay just opposite, had a residence here, the ruins of which, once surrounded with gardens, are to be seen upon it on the east side, near the present restaurant. The Government acquired it from them by arrangement during the war of 1812, and later by purchase in 1818, for military purposes. It ceded the park portion to the city in 1874.

Almost adjoining it, at the lower extremity, is Isle Ronde, a small, low island.

### III.—*Cemeteries.*

Out of regard for beauty of situation, the two great cemeteries, Protestant and Roman Catholic, lie behind the mountain.

**Mount Royal Cemetery,** the former, is one of the most lovely of Montreal's surroundings, occupying a secluded vale, landscape-gardened in perfect taste. It is approached either from the Mountain Park by a carriage road and by various paths over and around, or else by the highway called Mount Royal Avenue, on the north side, which leads through groves up to the principal Gate, a Gothic structure of stone. On entering, the Chapel is seen to the left, the Superintendent's Lodge to the right, in front lawns, flower beds and roads leading up the hill. To the right are the winter vaults. Finely situated to the left, far up on the hillside, is the range of family vaults, of which the Molson is the most conspicuous and the Tiffin the most tasteful. The former contains the remains of the Honourable John Molson. This cemetery is not old enough to contain many celebrities. There is, however, the quiet grave of the poet Heavysege, author of "Saul" and other dramas, and of a number of wierd and musical sonnets.

Adjoining Mount Royal Cemetery to the south, and situated on a separate face of the mountain, is the **Roman Catholic Cemetery**, less well-kept, but still containing things worth seeing. One of these sights is the Stations of the Cross; another the monument to the "patriots" (according to the side taken) of 1837, when a rebellion of a certain section of the French-Canadians against bureaucratic government took place; a third is the monument to Frs. Guibord, who was long refused burial in consecrated ground on account of membership in a Liberal Institute. The approach is by Cote des Neiges Road from Sherbrooke Street, over the mountain. On this road, at the height of the hill, is to be seen a ruin known as **Capitulation Cottage,** which is asserted, by tradition, to have been the headquarters of General Amherst when he occupied the heights on approaching to the siege of Montreal, then a small walled town miles away.

**The Hebrew Cemetery** is near the gate of the Protestant one. The Chaldaic letters and antique shapes of the tombstones attract the passing attention.

**The Old Military Cemetery** (on Papineau Street) is a relic of several generations ago, and contains the tombs of many well-known officers of the garrison.

## II.—PUBLIC BUILDINGS.

**The City Hall** is, externally, a large and exceedingly handsome example of modern French architecture, built of grey cut-stone, surmounted by a bold Mansard clock tower and heavy square corner turrets. The interior has a tolerably elegant appearance, produced by ranges of substantial Corinthian columns and galleries of natural wood. The Council Chamber is small and ineffective, however, and none of the offices remarkable. The debates are conducted in a mixture of French and English speeches, and the officials are nearly all French. The ground floor is given up to the police headquarters and the Recorder's Court. The tower affords one of the best views of the harbour and surroundings obtainable. In ascending it, one passes the Fire Alarm Signal Department, where the electric appliances are quite interesting.

Opposite is a long, low, cottage-built building of somewhat shabby mien, situated behind an old-fashioned stone fence. It is the **Château de Ramezay**, temporarily used for some of the lesser courts, but better known as a repertory of much provincial history. Two tablets upon it set forth a portion of its history. The one relates to its erection, about 1705, by Claude de Ramezay, Governor of Montreal, father of the de Ramezay who is somewhat maligned for surrendering Quebec, notwithstanding the impossibility of continuing its defence. The building later fell into the hands of the Compagnie des Indes Occidentales, and after the British conquest, was used for a considerable period as a residence for the English Governors when here. The other tablet relates to 1775, when the Americans held Montreal for a winter, and sent as commissioners to win over the Canadians, Benjamin Franklin, Samuel Chase and Charles Carroll. The former inscription is as follows: "Château de Ramezay. Built about 1705 by Claude de Ramezay, Governor of Montreal 1703. Headquarters of La Compagnie des Indes, 1745. Official residence of the British Governors after the Conquest. Headquarters of the American Army, 1775; of the Special Council, 1837." The latter tablet reads: "In 1775 this Château was the headquarters of the American Brigadier-General Wooster, and here in 1776, under General Benedict Arnold, the Commissioners of Congress, Benjamin Franklin, Samuel Chase, and Charles Carroll of Carrolton, held council." The vaults beneath are strong and substantial. The council-room is in the front, near the east-end entrance. It is oval at one end. There Franklin and his friends, and Benedict Arnold, retreating from Quebec, held their consultations, and Franklin's weapon, the printing-press, which was set up in the Château, must have been one of the chief subjects of discussion. The first printer of Montreal, Fleury Mesplet, was brought by him from Philadelphia, and was, in 1778, to found the earliest newspaper, the *Gazette*, a small sheet printed partly in French, partly English. His *Gazette* still flourishes as a morning paper—the third oldest journal in America.

From the same council-room Lord Elgin, having, after the rebellion of 1837, signed the unpopular Rebellion Losses Bill, went out to his carriage to be received by an angry populace with showers of rotten eggs and stones.

**The Court House,** or Palais de Justice, opposite the west side of the City Hall, is large, but uninteresting architectually.  In it are held the principal courts for the District of Montreal, and Americans usually experience some curiosity on seeing the robes and cocked hats of the Judges, the antique court costume and side sword of the Sheriff, the gowned bar and the Royal Arms, and in hearing the French cases.  Events connected with the historical tablets on the edifice are mentioned in describing Jacques Cartier Square.

In the vaults underneath old and valuable historical records are kept, with the general mass of judicial documents.  The Chief Justice of the Queen's Bench for the Province of Quebec is Sir Alex. Lacoste; the Chief Justice of the Superior Court is Sir Francis Johnson; the Sheriff is J. R. Thibaudeau.  As in the City Hall, nearly all the clerks are French.

The system of law in the Province of Quebec, it may be remarked, is, with little doubt, the best in the world.  It is substantially the highly-developed and scientific jurisprudence of the Roman Empire, improved by grafting the best parts of modern French and English law.

**The Post Office** on St. James Street, near the Place d'Armes, is a handsome building in French Renaissance style, but now much too small for the growing volume of business.  A couple of bas-reliefs, after designs from Flaxman, are inserted in the portico as mementoes of the old Bank of Montreal, which stood on the same site.  The office is open from 7.30 a.m. to 7 p.m. for general delivery.  There is a Savings' Bank attached, and nine branch offices are dispersed about town. In cases of doubt or difficulty, the Enquiry Department makes every reasonable effort to set matters right. The city letter rate is 2 cents ; for beyond the city limits the general rate is 3 cents.

**The Board of Trade** is a large and fine building, occupying the whole space between St. Peter and St. Nicholas on St. Sacrament Street. It is constructed of stone, with iron stairways throughout, is six stories in height, and has about 3,000 square feet of safety deposit vaults underneath. It contains the Board's exchange hall (about 4,000 feet in area), reading-room, council-room, stock exchange room, etc., the rest of the building being given up to offices.

**The Corn Exchange** stands opposite.

**The Custom House** has been referred to under Custom House Square. It might be added that the duties collected are about $10,000,000 a year, in round numbers.

**The Fraser Institute,** at the corner of Dorchester and University Streets, established by the will of the late Hugh Fraser, is the only free public library. It is an illustration of the difficulties of a radically-divided community in establishing general educational institutions. It possesses many valuable French works, the former property of the French Public Library Association, L'Institut Canadien, which it absorbed.

**The Mechanics' Institute,** on the corner of St. James and St. Peter Streets, also carries on a library and reading-room, not, however, free.

**The Natural History Museum** is a centre of a large

amount of valuable scientific work, and of several allied associations, such as the Microscopic Club. The *Canadian Record of Science* is published by the Society, and it has close relations with McGill University. A rare scientific library and many valuable specimens are stored in the building.

**The Art Gallery** is a small one, but its building is elegant externally, and the collection within is well chosen, without containing anything great or costly. It belongs to the Art Association, which was founded in 1860, but was able to do little until the bequest, some years later, by Benaiah Gibb, an art lover, of the site, with a small collection of paintings, several thousands of dollars and a lot of land. The Gallery was then erected. It has lately received a bequest of the estimated value of about $4,000 a year from the late J. W. Tempest, to be devoted to buying foreign pictures other than American or modern British. In the entrance hall a mural brass to the memory of Benaiah Gibb is placed. A reading-room is at the rear, study-room on the left, and the picture gallery overhead. The occasional loan exhibitions are the great feature, for at such times collections in Europe and the United States, and the private galleries of local men of taste, which, in Montreal, are exceeding rich, bring out treasures of the greatest interest and value. Such works as Millet's " Angelus," Breton's " Les Communiantes," Constant's " Herodiade," Watt's " Love and Death," and Turner's " Mercury and Argus " have been exhibited.

**The Drill Hall** is situated on Craig Street, opposite the Champ de Mars. It is a handsome limestone building, fitted with quarters for the various volunteer regiments. The main hall is the largest in the place, holding about 15,000 people.

**The Waterworks** are situated in the southern corner of the city. The large water-wheels and other machinery are of interest to engineers and those who like such things. The aim is to pump good water from the river above the city up to the two reservoirs on the mountain side, from which distribution takes place.

**The Bonsecours Market,** situated on the waterfront near Jacques Cartier Square, is one of the town sights on a market-day, for its scenes of French-Canadian provincial life. Thither on Tuesday and Friday the country *habitants* flock, with their little carts and their homespun clothing. Amid the jabber of Norman *patois*, and a preposterous haggling, worthy of Italy, over the "trente sous," the "neuf francs," or the "un ecu," one catches glimpses, through the jostling crowds, of piles of wooden shoes, brilliant strips of native rag-carpet, French home-made chairs or olive-wood rosaries and metal charms exposed for sale; and at Easter-tide the display of enormous beeves, decorated with paper roses, green, yellow and red, delight the hearts of the children, the peasants, and those who can still be both. The lover of human nature will observe a thousand studies of character in an early morning's push through these crowds. The building is a massive one of somewhat imposing aspect. It is surmounted by a large dome. The upper part was formerly the City Hall. It stands partly on the site of a house of Sir John Johnson, commander of the Indians during the American Revolution, and son of Sir William Johnson, "the Indian baronet;" and the site is also that of the Palace of the French Intendants. Many houses of the French period exist in this neighbourhood.

Next to it, at the north-east end, is the old church of **Notre Dame de Bonsecours,** which gave the market its name.

**St. Ann's Market,** on Foundling Street, is on the site of the Parliament Buildings, which stood here when Montreal was for a few years the capital of Canada. They were burnt in 1847, amid great uproar, by the same angry mob who rotten-egged Lord Elgin for his assent to the Rebellion Losses Bill. The oil portrait of the Queen was loyally cut out and saved during the fire by a young man named Snaith, and is now in the Parliament Buildings at Ottawa.

The name of Foundling Street adjoining was given on account of the finding there, in 1755, of an infant stabbed and floating in the ice of the little river which ran here. This it was which excited the compassion of Madame d'Youville, foundress of the Grey Nunnery, and led her to add to the work of that institution the care of abandoned infants, which has now become its principal work.

The other principal markets of the city are: St. Lawrence, St. Antoine and St. Jean Baptiste.

## CHAPTER IV.

### CHURCHES.

VILLE-MARIE having been founded as a community of missionaries and crusaders against the heathen, and the lords of the island having been a seminary of priests, one cannot be surprised to find the great majority of her streets and neighborhoods named after saints, from St. Gabriel and Ste. Cunegonde to St. Louis du Mile End, and to learn that religious devotion is strong to-day. It was the hope of the first settlers to create here a sort of ideal Catholic community—in an early writer's phrase, an "abode of angels." The ecclesiastical censorship, like the Connecticut Blue Law régime, had some good points, such as an earnest opposition to the evils of the brandy trade with Indians; but its weaknesses are amusingly pointed out by Baron La Hontan in his letters, about 1690, when, on entering his chamber in his lodgings at Montreal, he found that the Fathers had gone in without permission and torn up the classical romance with which he had been amusing his leisure.

New France was early established as an exclusively Catholic colony. Hence, in very great part arose its weakness and downfall. Had a liberal policy been carried out to Huguenot emigration, the leading French-Canadian historian has shown it probable that about 600,000 progressive citizens would have been added to its strength, instead of to the prosperity of England, Holland and Germany. As things actually went, New France was to the last feeble, struggling and backward, never able to conquer its Indian enemy, and reaching only the figure of about 70,000 inhabitants at the end of its existence in 1760.

An ecclesiastical aspect consequently survives. In the east-end of the city, along the Sherbrooke Street ridge, the whole town is dominated by a long range of convents and institutions. The priest, the friar, and even the cowled and bare-footed monk pass along the streets seen in their full costumes. Processions of nuns, too, in black, or grey, or buff, and of seminary students in cap, uniform and blue or green sash. Miracle pilgrimages leave the wharves for the shrines of St. Anne at Varennes or Beaupré. And at Christmas, Holy Week, Palm Sunday and All Saints' the churches are sights for large crowds of devotees and visitors.

Though a Huguenot company once owned the territory, and though a number of persons of Huguenot origin had taken part in its founding as officers and soldiers who were settled upon its lands, and though a number of child-captives taken during raids into New England were, from time to time, added to the population, Protestantism only became established with the

British conquest. For two generations more there was a constant movement, on the part of the British bureaucracy, to found some form of State Church, while the Anglican and Scotch Presbyterian Churches were privileged by law, and Crown Lands, called "Clergy Reserves," were set apart for their maintenance. The spirit of progress finally brought about the abolition of the system.

The marked contrast of the two religions, Protestant and Catholic, has had the effect of intensifying, while also liberalizing, the religious life of both, and also of making Montreal emphatically and strikingly a city of churches. The numerous spires and church edifices to be seen in every direction are remarked by every visitor.

I.—PROTESTANT CHURCHES.

*Anglican.*

**Christ Church Cathedral,** the most perfect church in Canada architectually, and, it is claimed with considerable reason, even in the whole of North America, is an exquisite example of the style known as Fourteenth-Century or Decorated Gothic. It was erected in 1859, under the guidance of the late Bishop Fulford, whose enthusiasm in matters of taste made him also the founder of the Art Association. A marble bust of him in the left transept perpetuates his connection with the church, and a beautiful spired monument, modelled after the celebrated Martyrs' Memorial at Oxford, keeps his memory green in the churchyard. From every point this edifice is a delight, so charming is each part and so perfectly harmonious the whole. It is built of rough grey limestone, embellished with facings of yellow Caen sandstone imported for the purpose, and carved in mediæval gurgoyles, corbels, pinnacles and other ornamental forms. It may be viewed from all sides with equal pleasure and artistic profit. The principal feature is the elegant stone spire, 211 feet high, with clock. The front, with carved porch, is also, though low, exceedingly attractive, and the octagonal Chapterhouse is in good taste. Internally, the massive carved pillars, well-pitched nave, deep choir, and a number of excellent stained-glass memorial windows, are worthy of notice. Likewise the exquisite stone font. Much of the wood and stone-carving about the building is said to be modelled from plants indigenous to Mount Royal. The music, both organ and choir, is generally good. The service is Low Church, and it may be remarked that the edifice, as a silent protest on that point, is placed with its chancel facing west instead of eastward.

**The Rectory** and Bishop's "Palace," known as "**Bishop's Court,**" are at the back of the grounds, and the Synod Hall adjoins on land next the Rectory. The latter is a neat Gothic structure of red pressed brick.

The original Christ Church, the immediate predecessor of this one, stood in Notre Dame Street, near St. Lambert Hill, where a tablet thus marks the site: "Site of Christ Church Cathedral, the first Anglican Church, 1814, burnt 1856." It, too, was a building of decided architectural taste.

The other Anglican Churches are: **St. George's,** which has been described under Dominion Square; **St. John the Evangelist** (Extreme Ritualist), on Ontario

Street, corner of St. Urbain Street; **St. James the Apostle** (High Church, with good choral litany Sundays at 4 p.m.), on St. Catherine, corner of Bishop Street; **St. Martin's** (Low), corner St. Urbain and Prince Arthur Streets; St. Stephen's, Trinity, St. Luke's, St. Jude's, St. Mary's, St. Thomas, etc., and L'Église du Redempteur (French).

*Presbyterian.*

ST. GABRIEL STREET CHURCH.

**Old St. Gabriel Church,** the quaint little building on St. Gabriel Street, adjoining the Champ de Mars and the Court House, has the honour of being the first Protestant Church erected in Montreal. A stone, recently removed, bore the date of erection, 1792. In its first years the Anglicans also worshipped here, the Protestant community of the small town being few and feeble. The congregations were largely military, from the garrison close by. Previous to its erection, the Presbyterians for several years worshipped in the Church of the Récollet Fathers, whom they, in grateful recognition on leaving, presented with a present of candles and a tun of communion wine. The congregation has its home, since 1886, on St. Catherine Street, near Phillips Square. But it should be said that the congregation of **Knox Church** is more nearly representative of the old St. Gabriel.

**St. Andrew's Church** (on Beaver Hall Hill) is, externally, a fine specimen of Early English or Scottish Gothic, with a well-proportioned spire, 180 feet high. It is a curiosity as being the only Canadian Presbyterian Church which has never left the Kirk of Scotland, and is sometimes styled " the Scotch Cathedral." The original St. Andrew's was built of stone, in 1814, on St. Helen Street.

**St. Paul's** (Dorchester Street West) possesses a beautiful pair of pinnacled towers, resembling those of Magdalen College at Oxford.

**Crescent,** further westward along Dorchester Street, is large and in early French Gothic, with fine spire.

The **American Presbyterian,** near the Windsor, on the same street, is a modern building, having the best organ among the Protestants of the city, and a large congregation.

The Presbyterians have three French Churches : St.

F

John's or Russell Hall, on St. Catherine Street, east of St. Lawrence Street; L'Eglise du Sauveur and L'Eglise de la Croix.

### *Methodist.*

**St. James Church,** on St. Catherine Street, a little east of Phillips Square, is one of the finest sacred edifices in Montreal in external appearance, and the largest Protestant temple except Christ Church Cathedral.

**The Dominion Square Methodist Church** has been referred to already.

Other large Methodist congregations are the Point St. Charles, the Second Methodist, the East End, the West End and the Douglas. There are two French ones, the First French and the Eglise Evangélique Méthodiste.

### *Baptists.*

The principal congregations are: The First Baptist (St. Catherine Street), Olivet (Mountain Street) and L'Oratoire (French), on St. George's Street. The position of the earliest place of worship of the denomination, on St. Helen Street, is marked by a inscription as follows: "Here stood the First Baptist Chapel of Montreal, 1831. The Rev. Jno. Gilmour, Pastor. Abandoned 1860."

### *Congregationalist.*

The principal churches are: Emmanuel (St. Catherine Street, corner of Stanley Street), Calvary (Guy Street) and Zion (Mance Street).

Some of the other churches are: The New Jerusalem Church, 25 Hanover Street; St. John's, German

Lutheran, 129 St. Dominique; the "Catholic Apostolic" or Irvingite, 35 Cathcart; St. Bartholomew's, Reformed Episcopal, 18 Beaver Hall Hill; the Plymouth Brethren, 32 University; Advent Christians, 2272 St. Catherine; and Salvation Army Barracks, Alexander Street. The Unitarians have a Lombard edifice, with fine spire, styled the Church of the Messiah, on Beaver Hall Hill. The pulpit chair is made of wood taken from the tower of old Notre Dame Church.

### II.—ROMAN CATHOLIC CHURCHES.

The Parish Church or **Nôtre Dame de Montréal** and **St. Peter's Cathedral** have been described under Place d'Armes and Dominion Square respectively.

**Nôtre Dame de Bonsecours,** opposite the east end of Bonsecours Market, is, historically, the most attractive of the local churches, except Notre Dame. In 1657, a wooden chapel, 30 by 40 feet, was erected here on a stone foundation, part of which remains to the present day. The land was given by Chomédy de Maisonneuve, founder of Ville-Marie. He also cut down the first trees and pulled them out of the wood. The church was built by order of the Sister Marie Bourgeoys, the earliest schoolmistress of the colony. The spot was then 400 yards outside the limits of the town. In 1675, the chapel being too small, another was built on the same site and of the same dimensions as the present one. The name Bonsecours was given on account of the escapes of the colony from the Iroquois. In 1754, a fire destroyed the second chapel, and, in 1771 the present church was constructed upon its foundations.

The stone foundations, therefore, of the present building go back to 1675. Till a few years ago it was a fine specimen of an old French provincial church, especially the elegant open tin-covered spire and gracefully-curved roof. The restoration-fiend, however, has played sad havoc with its outlines, putting on a new front, roof and spire, and improving away most of its beauty and uniqueness. There are still left a few suggestions of what it was—the inward-sloping walls, the statue of the Virgin on the rear peak of the roof, looking towards the water, a couple of the old paintings and altars, etc. The image of the Virgin is very old, and is supposed to have miraculous powers for the aid of sailors, many of whom yet pray to it. It was acquired by Sister Marie Bourgeoys from the Baron de Fancamp, a noble of Brittany, where it had been reputed for miracles. She, in consequence, brought it over, had the chapel built for it, and set it up where it stands, and where it has remained the patron of the French sailors for nearly two centuries and a half.

Another old little church, and one which bears its aspect of age quaintly, is reached by the gateway leading from Notre Dame Street to the Convent of the Congregation at St. Lambert Hill. It is a small, plain building of dark rough limestone, with round-arched doorway. The tablet upon it reads: "Nôtre Dame de Victoire, built in memory of the destruction of the fleet of Sir Hovenden Walker on the Isle aux Oeufs, 1711." This fleet sailed up the Gulf to attack Quebec at the one end of the colony, while the land forces of the British colonies were to advance from Albany against Montreal, under General Nicholson and Colonel Pieter Schuyler. A great storm in the Gulf shipwrecked the fleet, and frustrated the entire invasion. The French ascribed the catastrophe to the Virgin, and vowed her this chapel, which was erected seven years later, in 1718. The interior, now used as an engine-room, retains its original wood-panelling. The roof has been raised a story.

**The Gésu,** or **Jesuits' Church,** situated on Bleury Street, below St. Catherine, is one very much frequented by visitors on account of its frescoes and magnificent music. The former were the work of artists from Rome. The latter is chiefly heard on Sunday evenings, at which time, after the preaching, numbers crowd into the church to listen. The edifice is in that Italian modification known as Florentine Renaissance, or " the Jesuits' style." The design is that of the Church of the Gésu in Rome. The present towers are intended to be continued into spires. Internally, the delicate monochrome frescoes which adorn the walls and ceiling, reproduce the masterpieces of the modern German school : the Crucifixion, the Trinity, the Queen of Angels, the Holy Name of Jesus at the intersection of the transepts and nave, the Lamb of God, Jesus in the midst of the Doctors, Jesus with Mary and Joseph at Nazareth, Jesus blessing little children, the raising of Lazarus, Jesus as the Good Shepherd, Jesus appearing to St. Thomas after the Resurrection, scenes drawn from the history of the Jesuits. The fine oil paintings, by the Gagliardi brothers of Rome, are also worthy of inspection. In the basement there is a stage, and performances by the pupils of St. Mary's College adjoining are given, with lectures and other entertainments, from time to time, before the Cercle Catholique and similar organizations.

**St. Mary's College** is a large boys' school, presided over by the Jesuits. It possesses, among other things, things, a very rare collection of early historical documents and relics, collected largely by the learned Father Jones. In Canada the Order had a leading chapter of its history. From 1611, when Fathers Biard and Massé accompanied to Acadia some of the first settlers of New France, the members for a long time signalized themselves by extraordinary devotion and self-sacrifice, and were among the foremost in exploration of this continent. Eager for martyrdom, they pressed forward among the most savage tribes, overjoyed at being able to baptise the multitude of dying infants, and thus, as they believed, save the little ones' souls for heaven.

The passing by the Legislative Assembly of Quebec, with a handsome majority, among which were some Protestant votes, of the bill incorporating the Society of Jesus, makes a short sketch of their history in this province instructive and interesting.

From 1611, when the Rev. Fathers Biard and Massé accompanied to Acadia the first settlers of New France down to their expulsion in 1800, the members of the Society of Jesus have been active here. From the Atlantic shores of Acadia to the prairies of the far West, and from the frozen shores of Hudson Bay to the sunny plains of Louisiana, the Fathers laboured, and Canadian history is full of their doings. The blood of Fathers Brebœuf and Lallemant, burnt by the

Iroquois in 1649; of Daniel, shot by arrows and musket balls in 1648; of Jogues, struck down by a hatchet in 1646; of Garnier, butchered in 1649; of Chabanel, drowned by an apostate Huron in 1649; of Garreau, Pierron and a host of others attest the hardships and dangers of their work.

In 1772 the Pope suppressed the order, and when the decree was received in Quebec, the then Governor, Lord Dorchester, acting upon instructions from the minister, prevented the Bishop from publishing it, and it was privately communicated to the Jesuits by the Bishop. The Order became extinct in 1800 by the death of the last Jesuit, Father Cazot, who was allowed by the British Government to peacefully enjoy his estates till his death.

The suppression of the order was lifted in 1814, and in 1839, after an absence of nearly forty years, they returned to Canada.

Though it was a Jesuit, Father Vimont, who celebrated the first mass in Ville-Marie, their influence was much more felt at Quebec than Montreal. There they became zealously autocratic, driving away the Order of Récollets (who, having been the first on the ground, had called in their aid), and carried on, through Montmorency de Laval, the first Bishop in Canada, a long and heated feud with the Sulpicians of Montreal.

Here, their early church and residence was on Jacques Cartier Square, adjoining what is now the Champ de Mars, and forming together three sides of a quadrangle, opening towards Notre Dame Street. The reader may turn for fuller information to Parkman's "Jesuits in New France."

On St. Helen Street, just adjoining the corner of Notre Dame Street, there stood, till a few years ago, a church and monastery, which gave its name to a gate and whole quarter of the French town—the quarter and gate of the Récollets. A tablet erected there bears the words: "Here stood, until 1866, the **Church and Monastery of the Récollet Fathers**, 1692, in which the Anglicans from 1764 to 1789, and the Presbyterians from 1791 to 1792, worshipped." It was also the first Parish Church for the Irish Catholics of Montreal, from 1830 to 1847.

**Nôtre Dame de Lourdes** is another visitors' church. It stands near the corner of St. Denis and St. Catherine Streets, and its façade is of marble. Concerning this church, I cannot do better than condense the description given by a very competent critic, Mr. A. E. Dawson, heretofore Chairman of the Board of Arts: "This church has been built and adorned with one idea—that of expressing in visible form the dogma of the Immaculate Conception of the Virgin Mary. The architecture of the church is Byzantine and Renaissance, such as may be seen at Venice. It consists of a nave with narrow aisles, a transept and a choir. The choir and the transept are terminated by a circular and domed apses, and a large central dome rises at the intersection of the transept. The large dome is 90 feet high, the total length of the church 102 feet. . . . . The first picture on the roof of the nave represents the promise of the Redemption made to Adam and Eve.

They are prostrated before the Lord, who addresses the Serpent—'She shall bruise thy head.' The next panel is the sacrifice of Abraham. The third represents the arrival of Rebecca before Isaac. The fourth, which is over the choir, is Jacob blessing his children. On the right of the nave are the prophets who have prophesied of the Virgin—Isaiah, Jeremiah, David, Micah. On the left are types of the Virgin—Sarah, Rebecca, Rachel, Ruth. The artist then proceeds to show the Roman view of the realization of these promises—the Salutation of Elizabeth and the Nativity—in the transepts, with the Greek and Latin Fathers respectively who have magnified Mary. The choir contains the exposition of the Dogma proper. The statue over the altar, and which strikes the eye immediately on entering the church, is symbolic of the doctrine. It represents the Virgin in the attitude usually attributed to this subject by the Spanish painters—the hands crossed on the breast. She is standing on the clouds, and the text illustrated is Rev. xii. 1 : 'A woman clothed with the sun, and the moon under her feet.' The light thrown down from an unseen lamp is to represent the clothing with the sun."

"The artist, M. Bourassa, must have the credit," says Mr. Dawson, "of working out his exposition with force and unity. Some of the painting is exceedingly good. The decoration of the church in gold and colours, arabesque and fifteenth-century ornament, is very beautiful and harmonious. . . . . We have dwelt at length upon this building, because it is the only one of its kind in America."

Mr. Dawson is himself, we believe, the originator of the project of a French-Canadian school of church decorators, whose field should be the Roman Catholic Churches of the North American continent, and of which the Board of Arts and Manufactures has, under his guidance, established a respectable beginning at Montreal.

Beneath the church is a chapel representing the alleged apparition of the Virgin to the young girl Bernadette Soubirons in a grotto near Lourdes, France, in 1858, at which time a miracle-working fountain is said to have commenced to gush out of the rock, and still continues making miraculous cures.

**L'Eglise St. Jacques** near by, stands on the site of the former Roman Cathedral, and is a highly fashionable French place of worship. Its spire is the highest in the city, slightly exceeding the towers of Notre Dame. The new transept is a handsome piece of Gothic.

**St. Patrick's,** "the Irish Cathedral," on St. Alexander Street, is a grand specimen of early French Gothic, both in and out. The quaint stone façade, with rose window, and the massive but still open spire, are truly notable for their combination of grace and power.

Other notable Roman Catholic Churches are: The Church of the Sacred Heart, the Chapel of the Congregation Nuns, St. Henri Parish Church, Ste. Cunegonde Parish Church.

### III.—JEWISH SYNAGOGUES.

At this point we ought not to overlook the earliest synagogue. Jews appear in Montreal very soon after the Conquest (at least, as early as 1765, and probably with the British entry). Their first synagogue building was on Notre Dame Street, west of the Court House Square, where the tablet reads: "Here stood the first Synagogue of Canada, erected in 1777, A.M. 5557, by the Spanish and Portuguese Jewish Congregation 'Shearith Israël;' founded 1768."

There are now five synagogues in the place. That of the Spanish rite on Stanley Street is remarkable as a specimen, especially within, of Ægypto-Judean architecture. Four magnificent stone Egyptian columns support the portico.

## CHAPTER V.

### CHARITABLE AND RELIGIOUS INSTITUTIONS.

WERE, again, the sharp division of Roman Catholic and Protestant comes in, though the charity of some of the institutions is broader than their denominational limits. There is nothing of which Montreal can be prouder than the large-heartedness of many of her wealthy citizens. There are only two kinds of men worth considering—the generous and the mean. Montreal has had, like other places, some conspicuously mean millionaires; but no town has had a greater proportion of generous ones, and these she delights to keep remembered.

#### I.—PROTESTANT.

**The Victoria Hospital,** though new, stands at the head of all. The gift of two citizens, Sir Donald Smith and Lord Mount-Stephen, it dominates the city from the top of University Street, on a shoulder of Mount Royal, at the eastern edge of the park. It is a huge and most picturesque building of uncut limestone, resembling some castellated Scotch palace. The style, in fact, is Scottish Baronial. The cost was over $1,000,000, apart from the land, which was contributed by the city. The Hospital occupies one of the most commanding situations possible. On approach, it is found to consist of a magnificent main building situated across a court-yard, the sides of which are formed by long, tall, narrow wings boldly standing forward, their appearance of height enhanced by a pair of tall turrets at the front corners of each, and also by the slope of the hillside. The interior is constructed and managed on the most modern hospital plans and principles.

**The General Hospital,** on Dorchester Street, at the corner of St. Dominique, is the most widely-venerated establishment. Its tradition, though supported almost entirely by Protestant contributions, is that of an open door, and kind relief to all sufferers, without regard to race or creed. It was established in 1821. The daily average of in-door patients is about 170; of out-door, about 700.

**The Protestant House of Industry and Refuge** is the head centre for distribution of relief to the Protestant poor, and is carried on by a committee of citizens. It has a country home for the aged and infirm at Longue Pointe. It is situated on Dorchester Street, east of Bleury.

**The Western Hospital,** 1269 Dorchester Street West, is the leading establishment for diseases of women.

**The Mackay Institute for Protestant Deaf Mutes** (also for the blind), on Cote St. Luc Road, Cote St.

Antoine; incorporated 1869. One of the most beneficent and interesting of institutions. Six teachers, forty deaf and five blind children inmates.

**The Hervey Institute,** Mountain Street, below Dorchester, is a children's home. So are the **Protestant Infants' Home,** 508 Guy Street, and the **Protestant Orphan Asylum** (established 1822), 2409 St. Catherine Street.

**The Boys' Home,** 117 Mountain Street, below St. Antoine, does an excellent work of rescue and training.

The other Protestant Institutions are: The W.C.T.U., St. Catherine Street, foot of Victoria Street; Y.W.C.A., 75 Drummond Street; St. Andrew's Home (Scotch), 403 Aqueduct Street; St. George's Home (English), 139 St. Antoine Street; the Montreal Maternity Hospital, 93 St. Urbain Street; the Women's Protective Immigration Society, Osborne Street, near Mountain; the Ladies' Benevolent Society, 31 Berthelet Street; the Canadian Society for Prevention of Cruelty to Animals, 198 St. James Street; the Society for Protection of Women and Children, Temple Building; the Irish Protestant Benevolent Society, 691 Dorchester Street; the Protestant Hospital for the Insane, Verdun; St. Margaret's Home, 660 Sherbrooke Street; Montreal Sailors' Institute, 320 Commissioners Street; the Baron de Hirsch Institute (Jewish); the Hebrew Benevolent.

**The Y.M.C.A.** has been described under Dominion Square.

II.—ROMAN CATHOLIC.

**The Hotel Dieu** (Hotel Dieu St. Joseph de Ville-Marie), the oldest and vastest of the Roman Catholic

Hospitals, is, of course, a great nunnery as well. Its long front, large stone garden-walls and tin-covered roofs and dome, infallibly catch the eye near the head of Park Avenue, and bordering on the east corner of Mount Royal Park. The nunnery is on one side of the central chapel, the hospital on the other. It was founded, about 250 years ago, in 1644, by the Duchesse de Bullion, "the unknown benefactress," one of the aristocratic circle of the Association of Montreal, who gave to found it a sum of 42,000 livres, which, though she was entirely ignorant of the real needs of the place, she insisted should not be used for any other purpose. Mlle. Mance and the other practical people on the spot could see no earthly use in diverting such a sum from the Huron mission and other needs of the colony to a building without prospect of occupation. The idea had been that of Monsieur de la Dauversière, the collector of taxes who, with M. Olier of the Seminary, had planned out this extraordinary colony on a visionary foundation. In a year or so, however, the Iroquois began to attack the place, and then the hospital turned out of use. It has ever since continued to bless immense multitudes of sick. The original building was erected on St. Paul Street, not far from Custom House Square. It was "60 feet long by 24 feet wide, with a kitchen, a chamber for Mlle. Mance, others for servants, and 2 large apartments for the patients. It was amply provided with furniture, linen, medicines and all necessaries; and possessed 2 oxen, 3 cows, and 20 sheep. A small oratory of stone was built adjoining. The enclosure was 4 arpents (acres) in length." It was fortified by palisades. The Antiquarian Society's tablet on the front wall of the present institution relates the story of its establishment in its present place: " Hotel Dieu de Ville-Marie, founded in 1644 by Jeanne Mance. Transferred in 1861 to this land, given by Benoit and Gabriel Basset. Removal of the remains of Jeanne Mance and 178 nuns, 1861." The *religieuses* of the Hotel Dieu are known as "the Black Nuns." Such of them as have taken the vows of "the cloistered" never leave the premises.

Mlle. Mance, the foundress, was an enthusiast of the extremest type. Her childhood itself is said to have been taken up with extraordinary vows, and miraculous visions and portents were with her to the end of her life. Her arm was cured of palsy at the grave of Olier; visions pointed out to her her mission at Ville-Marie. Hither she came, with three female servants, the only women in the company. She died in 1673, and was buried in the Hotel Dieu; but her heart was to have been placed as a relic in the sanctuary lamp of Notre Dame. A flood, however, 22 years later, which destroyed the old Hotel Dieu, carried it off.

**The Grey Nuns' Hospital** takes its current name from the grey costume of its community. More even than the Hotel Dieu, this institution strikes one by its monastic vastness and severity of outline, extending over great part of a large four-square street-block. It was founded, in 1747, by Madame d'Youville (Marie Marguerite du Frost de la Jemmerais), the widow of an officer. Many curious objects, made by, or belonging to, her, and illustrating the state of her times, belong to the institution, such as delicate embroidery and her enamelled clasp-knife.

The nuns are said to have received their name at first in hatred, for malice was rife against them and the foundress, on the part of the Governor of the town and the leading inhabitants, from their foundation, and they were accused, among the common people, of the use of alcohol and other atrocious qualities. This arose from the old Hospital General, founded in 1694, and until then conducted inefficiently by monks, having been placed under her direction by the Bishop. The people took the part of the monks. Her kind treatment of the English prisoners shows her to have been an estimable woman, and won afterwards the esteem of the conquerors.

The nuns are always glad to receive visitors, of whom a great many attend. Every New Year's there is a formal reception, when the sisters stand in two rows and receive all-comers, after an old custom. Great numbers of infants are left by unknown parties at the institution, the immense majority of which, unfortunately, die in a short time. It is also an asylum for the sick, maimed, infirm, aged, insane and desolate of all sects. In 1870 they built the present vast stone building. It contains more than 320 rooms. There are over 100 sisters and about 100 novices. Support is principally derived from the rents of houses and lands belonging to the Order and the united industries of the Sisterhood.

The daughter of the celebrated Ethan Allen, the founder of Vermont State, and leader of "The Green Mountain Boys," died a member of this order. A tradition is related that during her girlhood, long before her conversion to Catholicism, she was pursued by a terrible monster, who attacked her as she was walking by a river. She was saved by an old man, whose features and appearance were thenceforth vividly stamped upon her memory. She was afterwards sent to a convent in Montreal for her education, and became a Romanist. Returning, she visited this convent among some others. She was struck by a picture of St. Joseph, and stood in front of it gazing. "There," exclaimed she, pointing to it, "is he, my preserver!" and went on to explain; and thereupon she decided to take the vows of the Grey Nuns! So runs the tale. The picture remains there still.

In the corner of the grounds at Dorchester Street a tall cross of red-stained wood is to be seen, to which a history attaches, called **The Story of the Red Cross.** The popular narrative is that it marks the grave of a notorious highwayman, who robbed and murdered *habitants* returning from Montreal to St. Laurent and the back country by way of Dorchester Street, which was, in French times, the only highway west of St. Lawrence Street through the forest. This story is somewhat incorrect.* Belisle, the man in question, was not a highway robber; his crime was housebreaking and a double murder. He lived on Le Grand Chemin du Roi, now called Dorchester Street, near this spot. On the other side of the road, and a little higher up, Jean Favre and his wife Marie Anne lived, who were reputed to have money in their house and to be well off.

---

* On the authority of P. S. Murphy, Esq., of the Antiquarian Society.

Belisle formed the envious project of robbing his neighbour, and accordingly, one dark night, broke into the house and fired his pistol at Favre, which, however, only wounding, he stabbed him to death with a large hunting knife. Favre's wife rushed in to help her husband. Belisle plunged the knife into her breast, and then despatched her by a blow of a spade. He was suspected, and soon after arrested, tried and convicted. The terrible punishment of *breaking alive* was then in force under French law. Belisle was condemned to "torture ordinary and extraordinary," and then "to have his arms, legs, thighs and reins broken alive on a scaffold to be erected in the market-place of this city" (the present Custom House Square); "then put on a rack, his face towards the sky, to be left to die." The awful sentence was carried out to the letter, his body buried in Guy Street, and a Red Cross erected to mark the spot. The present cross has been moved back a few feet because of a widening of the street.

The *old* Grey Nunnery is situated in its stone-walled yard, now used for coal, near the foot of McGill Street. The original edifice has been lately removed, but the larger erections remain still. The walls and remains of the chapel can be seen from behind, incorporated in warehouses and stores.

**Notre Dame Hospital,** on Notre Dame Street, near Dalhousie Square, is a much smaller institution than the foregoing, but has, like the General Hospital, an open door for all creeds, though managed by Roman Catholics.

Other large establishments are:

**The Asile de la Providence** (St. Catherine Street), under the care of an order of nuns, who, besides caring for the sick, aged and orphans, have the largest Insane Asylum of the Province in their house at Longue Pointe, below the city.

**The Institution for Deaf Mutes,** St. Denis Street.

**The Deaf and Dumb Institution.**

**The Bon Pasteur Convent,** Sherbrooke Street.

**The Roman Catholic Orphan Asylum,** St. Catherine Street.

**St. Patrick's Orphan Asylum,** Dorchester Street, near Beaver Hall Hill. About 150 inmates.

St. Bridget's Home, Lagauchetiere Street, near Beaver Hall; St. Joseph's Asylum, 60 Cathedral Street; Nazareth Asylum and Institute for the Blind, 2023 St. Catherine Street; Home for the Aged of the Little Sisters of the Poor, 109 Forfar Street.

## UNIVERSITIES.

The celebrated **McGill University** is one of the finest in America. The grounds are extensive, tree-grown and enclosed with a light, black, iron fence, and the main building, to which an avenue leads from the lodge gates, stands well back on a rise in the distance. To the right and left, partly concealed by trees, are the other buildings of the University. The large and beautiful Greek building to the left is the Redpath Museum; on its left is the affiliated Presbyterian College; below it the new Library; further, across McTavish Street, the Congregational College; above the Museum, the

MONTREAL AFTER 250 YEARS.   85

small round tower is the Observatory.  In front of the main building, with its Doric portico, is the grave of James McGill ; on the right, the Medical College, towards the rear ; Ferrier Hall (the Methodist affiliated College), hidden by the other buildings ; then the great McDonald Technical School ; nearer still, the handsome ~~Workman~~ Laboratory of Physics ; and on the extreme left, forming the corner of University Street, the Donalda Ladies' Department.  The foreground is occupied by college campus and walks.  Behind the whole, Mount Royal rises prominently as a refreshing green background.

The institution is entirely the result of the private munificence of a succession of large-hearted merchants. The first and most honoured was the founder, James McGill, one of the old Scotch fur traders, who, in 1813, bequeathed £10,000 and his lands of sixty-four acres here, known as the Manor of Burnside, to the Royal Institution for the Advancement of Learning.  His town residence and warehouse was in a building opposite the City Hall, which bears a tablet of the Antiquarian Society.  His country house of Burnside stood a short distance down McGill College Avenue, where the synagogue is built.  His portrait in the college represents him as a stout, pleasant-tempered man, of superior intelligence, in a powdered queue.

The blue-stone monument over his remains in McGill College Grounds reads as below.  Part of the letters seem to have been re-cut on removal from the old Dorchester Street Cemetery, and in doing this a mistake has occurred in saying the " 4th " instead of the " 1st "

Battalion. "To the memory of the Honourable James McGill, a native of Glasgow, North Britain, and being several years a representative of the City of Montreal in the Legislative Assembly, and Colonel of the 4th Battalion of Montreal Militia, who departed this life on the 19th day of December, 1813, in his 69th year. In his loyalty to his sovereign, and in ability, integrity, industry and zeal as a magistrate, and in the other relations of public and private life, he was conspicuous; his loss is accordingly sincerely and greatly regretted." Lower down, near the base, we read: "This monument, and the remains which it covers, were removed from the old Protestant Cemetery, Dorchester Street, and placed here in grateful remembrance of the founder of this University; 25 June, 1875."

One Desrivières, his step-son, whom he had generously made his heir, did his best to thwart the bequest by refusing possession of either the land or the money, and even had the singular ill-faith to plead at law that the trustees had not built the college within the time—ten years—stated in the will. The judge severely commented on his conduct, compelled him to render up both money and land, and the institution was begun. Its early fortunes were so varied, that it was forced to sacrifice the most of its land, which extended down to Dorchester Street, and at one time it is said that only the tenacity of a man of superior temperament and intelligence, Professor William Turnbull Leach, later Archdeacon of Montreal, kept it in existence. It has now possessions valued at several millions. Morrin College, Quebec, and St. Francis College, Richmond, are colleges of the University. The University is undenominational Protestant. Its faculties are : Arts, Medicine, Applied Science, Law and Comparative Anatomy. Of these, the Medical is most widely celebrated. The entire number of students is about 1,000, sending out annually a stream of educated men who achieve the highest positions. The Principal is Sir William Dawson.

**The Redpath Museum,** especially the great hall, is finished and arranged very beautifully in Greek spirit. Among other things, it contains on exhibition a magnificent geological collection, the work, in large part, of Sir William Dawson ; the model of a gigantic megatherium, a weird collection of wood-carvings by the Thlinkit Indians of the Pacific Coast, the exquisite shell collection of the late Dr. P. P. Carpenter, aboriginal skulls and remains from the site of Montreal and other localities, and the skelton of a whale caught in the St. Lawrence opposite the city.

**The Redpath Library** is a recent gift capable of holding 150,000 volumes. It contains about 35,000, and has spacious reading-rooms for men and women, and study-rooms of the best construction, with other appliances. Though small in number of books, it is especially rich in works relating to Canada, in historical pamphlets, and in scientific works. The fac-simile of Domesday Book and its iron chest is a curiosity. Besides this general library, others of considerable value are found in the Medical College, the Faculty of Applied Science, and the various Theological Colleges, that of Morrice Hall (Presbyterian) being most notable.

**The McDonald Technical Building** should be gone over. It is one of the best-equipped buildings for technical training in America.

**The ~~Workman~~ Physics Building** is also very interesting.

The amusements of the students are mainly football, tennis, cricket and general athletics. The campus and tennis-grounds are good for these purposes.

**Bishops' University** (Episcopal) and **Victoria University** are represented in Montreal by Medical Colleges only.

**Laval University,** of Quebec (French Roman Catholic), is in process of establishing itself here, and will probably do so on a large scale. It has a flourishing law school, and is taking over the Victoria Medical College, but has not yet erected buildings.

### OTHER EDUCATIONAL INSTITUTIONS.

The duality of Protestant and Catholic is even more sharply defined in educational institutions than in benevolent. The Provincial Council of Public Instruction is divided into two—a Protestant and a Catholic branch, and taxation is separate. Local management is in the hands of separate Boards of Protestant and Catholic Commissioners. The chief schools under the former in Montreal are the High School for Boys and High School for Girls, which occupy different portions of the High School Building on Peel Street, and the Normal School, for training of teachers, on Belmont Street. The number of pupils in the first is about 250; in the second, about 300; and in the last, about 100.

The Boys' High School was originally the Royal Grammar School, and afterwards a department of McGill University. There are in the city sixteen common schools under the Protestant Commissioners, besides Trafalgar Institute for Women and many good private schools, such as the College of Commerce (Drummond Street) and the Business College (Victoria Square).

The principal schools of the Roman Catholic Commissioners are the **Plateau Street Academy** and the Ecole Normale on Sherbrooke Street, both excellent French schools, occupying noble buildings. They are for boys alone, Roman Catholic girls being sent to convents.

The Catholic Commissioners have, besides, a number of other schools under their care. Altogether, the city contains 4 Catholic "colleges," 36 "academies," 31 "schools."

Some of the French establishments are interesting from their historical associations or foreign air. Those named *collèges* are of the nature of high schools.

**The Séminaire de St. Sulpice,** or **Grand Seminary,** for the training of priests, has been already described under Place d'Armes.

Its junior branch, the **Collège de Montreal,** or **Petit Séminaire,** is situated on Sherbrooke Street West, on "the Priests' Farm," an ancient property of the Order. Its large buildings are built upon the site of one of the earliest edifices of Montreal, the country house of the Grand Seminary, known as the Maison des Messieurs, or Fort de la Montagne, around which the village of the

Indian converts was placed. The Maison des Messieurs, now represented by two historic towers, standing as relics of a mediæval past, was a large rough old edifice of plastered stone, three stories high in the centre and two elsewhere, surmounted by roofs resembling those of the present Grand Seminary, pinnacled and curved in the inimitable old French roof-curves. An extensive

THE OLD SEMINARY TOWERS.

stone wall enclosed it for purposes of fortifications, while the pair of towers formed part of the wall in front, and between them was the entrance. In a walled enclosure adjoining, to the eastward, was the Indian village; in another, to westward, large gardens. One of the old towers, in very early times, was used as a chapel of the Indian mission established here, the other being used as a school. A tablet in the former reads in

French: "Here rest the mortal remains of François Thoronhiongo, Huron; baptized by the Reverend Père Brebœuf. He was by his piety and by his probity the example of the Christians and the admiration of the unbelievers: he died, aged about 100 years, the 21st April, 1690."

What untold histories, traditions and reminiscences doubtless died with this centenarian savage! And baptized by Père Brebœuf! The latter was a hero of one of the most dreadful martyrdoms recorded. In 1649, he and Father Lalement, both Jesuits, were tortured to death by Iroquois with every cruelty devisable.

In the other, "the Schoolmistress of the Mountain," an Indian sister of great repute for sainthood, taught, and to her a memorial reads as follows: "Here rest the mortal remains of Marie Therèse Gannensagouas, of the Congregation of Notre Dame. After having exercised during 13 years the office of schoolmistress at the Mountain, she died in reputation of great virtue, aged 28 years, the 25th November, 1695."

Over the door of the western wing one reads: "**Hic evangelibantur Indi**"—" Here the Indians were evangelized."

A tablet on the wall in front, on Sherbrooke Street, records the founding of the Indian mission in 1677, and the facts concerning the Towers.

Some distance along the wall eastwards is still another tablet, marking the position of General Amherst's army at the time of the surrender of the town to the English power.

Within the grounds may often be seen crowds of

boys uniformed in black frock coats, blue sashes and peaked caps, playing ball or tennis in their high stationary tennis-court, or discoursing music as a well-equipped band. Within the college the theatre would be found an important amusement. The curriculum is divided into two parts: theology and philosophy. Boys are taken from early years upwards. In the last years they choose either to study for the priesthood or for other occupations, and thus separate. The course is based largely on the classical languages, declamation and the philosophy of Thomas Aquinas. The number of pupils and students of all parts of the institution is about 450.

Further up on the hill, for the Seminary here owns an immensely valuable and large tract, stand two other buildings, one an old country house of the order, with grove of trees and ornamental pond, the other, higher up, a handsome new institution for the headquarters of the Order.

**St. Mary's College,** the school of the Jesuit Fathers, has been referred to in connection with the Church of the Gésu, which it adjoins, on Bleury Street.

**The Board of Arts Schools,** on St. Gabriel Street, opposite the Champ de Mars, should be added as meriting inspection.

**The Christian Brothers' Schools** are on Coté Street.

For girls, the great convents are those of the Nuns of the Congregation, Mount St. Mary and the Hochelaga Convent. Their curriculum consists chiefly of the accomplishments: music, sewing, religious instruction, deportment, etc.

**The Nuns of the Congregation,** or Sisters of the Congregation de Notre Dame, are the great teaching order, having convents in most of the large villages of the Province and many others throughout Canada and the United States. They have here their two most interesting establishments of the kind, being the older and newer mother houses of the community. Both buildings are of historic interest. The older is in the lower town, and reached by a gateway from Notre Dame Street, opposite St. Lambert Hill; the newer is a vast and magnificent structure, whose group of spires appears prominently on the extreme south-westerly slope of Mount Royal.

One of the most famous pioneers of French Canada, Marguerite Bourgeoys, the earliest school teacher of the colony, a devoted and sensible person, founded the order. She is greatly revered in the history of her people. Her first school was established at Boucherville, on the opposite side of the St. Lawrence, at a point now marked by a memorial inscribed cross. On entering the quaint gateway from Notre Dame Street, one sees to the right the gable of the curious little building of stone, described previously as Notre Dame de Victoire, one of the most antique relics of Montreal's past.

Passing on, one sees ahead a cut-stone church, of no great size, but bearing an inscription stating that it is erected on the site of one built in 1693 by Marguerite Bourgeoys herself. A view to the left from this point shows the convent surrounding its court-yard in the shape of ranges of buildings of an ancient appearance.

Within are many quaint relics, among others a curious contemporary painting in black and white of Mdlle. Le Ber. A tablet reads: "Congregation of Notre Dame, founded by Marguerite Bourgeoys. Convent built 1686. Jeanne Le Ber lived here solitary from 1695 to 1714."

The newer mother-house, called **Villa Maria**, is, as has been stated, on the Mountain-side at Cote St. Antoine, where it is especially prominent at the hour when its spires cross the sunset. A magnificent chapel is the chief attraction. There are large grounds, which originally belonged to an old family named Monk, whence the name Monklands, and afterwards were the place of residence of several of the Governor-Generals. Their dwelling is incorporated among the new buildings. The number of sisters here is about 270; but the order has 105 establishments, with some 1,200 sisters and about 25,000 pupils.

**The Hochelaga Convent** and **Mount St. Mary** are convents of a similar nature, but much less splendor or interest. A number of American pupils are boarders.

RELIGIOUS ORDERS.

Several communities of old-world monks and cloistered nuns are represented in Montreal.

**The Trappists,** though only occasionally seen as single members on the streets, are a most interesting Order, exhibiting a perfect picture of a mediæval community of monks. They wear a long coarse brown woollen robe and cowl, shave the head and observe perpetual silence, except when spoken to by their Superior. Their specialty is agriculture, and their headquarters their monastery and beautiful farm of 1,000 acres at Oka, some 30 miles above the city. There every person is hospitably received and kept as long as he desires to stay, on the understanding that he does so for religious meditation. The curious mediæval meals of bread and vegetables twice a day, the wondrous old psalters used by each monk in the chapel, the strange silence, the flagellation scourges, cells, rude beds, and the intense absorption of some of the devotees make up a fascinating sight.

**The Carmelites** are nuns of a still severer regime, and have their convent at Hochelaga. Its walls are very high, and the sisters (who are few in number) have, by the vows of this order, renounced the sight of the outside world for the remainder of their lives. The lives of cloistered nuns, even when of teaching or hospital orders, are always sad : what, then, must those of these sisters be ?

### SOCIETIES.

*Literature, Science, Art, History, Antiquarianism.*

**The Natural History Society** was mentioned in connection with its **Museum.**

**The Numismatic and Antiquarian Society** is the most active of the historical associations. It was founded December 15, 1862, under the title of " The Numismatic Society of Montreal," with a membership of French and English gentlemen—a dual racial character which has happily characterized it ever since, and makes it one of the not least effective influences of harmony and goodwill in the community. In 1866 the name was changed to its present title, and in 1869 an act of incorporation was obtained. In the Natural History Museum the society preserves and adds to its considerable collection of coins, medals, maps, books and manuscripts. In the Caxton celebration year it held a memorable exhibition of rare books; in 1887, a unique exhibition of historical portraits, the catalogue of which remains a list of value to historians; the Maisonneuve Monument is its proposal; and the Historical Tablets, suggested by one of its members, have been erected by this society. It publishes the valuable *Antiquarian Journal.*

**The Société Historique,** another old society, has also done valuable work, re-published a number of most rare manuscripts, including Dollier de Casson's " Histoire du Montréal," and has in hand a proposed monument for the landing-place of Maisonneuve, to consist of a granite obelisk, with inscription. The society contains, among other possessions, the **Sabretache** portfolio of Commander Jacques Viger, which furnished material to the historians Parkman and Kingsford.

**The Society for Historical Studies** published *Canadiana* for some years, and assisted in disseminating the love of history.

**The Society of Canadian Literature** opened up the field of Canadian letters, and still exists for occasional work of the same nature.

The Folk-Lore Club, the Shakespeare Club, the Microscopical Society, the **Horticultural Society, Mendelssohn Choir, Philharmonic Society,** are some names of the better-known associations.

## SPORTS, PASTIMES, THEATRES, CLUBS, ETC.

### *Athletics.*

Athletics are the delight of Montreal. Here alone are the Winter Carnival and Ice Palace possible—at least, at their best. Here, too, the Indian pleasures of the lacrosse, the toboggan and the snowshoe, associated with the bright old *voyageur* blanket costume, are in their native air; here the Scotch curling-rinks took root generations ago as solidly-established institutions; while cricket, football, tennis, fox-hunting, fishing, shooting, rowing, yachting, golf and all the Anglo-Saxon games are devotedly pursued. The use of the blanket costume for purposes of sport is attributed by some to the enthusiasm of the British army colony; but there is no doubt but that it is a legacy from the Old North-Westers.

**The Montreal Amateur Athletic Association** is the largest organization of the athletic interest. It has some 2,000 members, a well-equipped club-house and headquarters, and a large stretch of superb grounds on the west edge of the city. The association had its beginning, in 1840, in the shape of the Montreal Snowshoe Club, now familiarly known as "the Old Tuque Blue," from the blue woollen *habitant's* liberty cap, worn as a part of the costume. The club, in consequence of its long standing, preserves a rich display of trophies in its rooms. It has always thrown its influence on the side of temperance, public progress and national spirit. It has at times organized vigorous movements against attempts to establish saloons within its district;

has given large numbers of its members to the militia, especially in times of danger; and was the originator and mainstay of the winter carnivals and of the snowshoe concert. In winter its snowshoers tramp over the Mountain or to Lachine, and sometimes farther, ending up by a jolly dance and supper; in summer, the games of lacrosse on its suburban grounds absorb the same interest. Lacrosse, as played on these grounds, is the most spectacular game existing. Its simplicity, the rapidity and grace of flight of the ball, and the lightning changes of fortune or strokes of skill, immediately enchain the attention and excite the blood.

The clubs now included in the Association are: The Montreal Snowshoe Club, the Montreal Lacrosse Club, the Montreal Bicycle Club, the Tuque Bleue Toboggan Club, the Montreal Football Club, the Montreal Gymnasium, the M.A.A.A. Dramatic Club, the Cinderella Club, the Montreal Fencing Club, the Montreal Hockey Club, the Tuque Bleue Skating Rink, the Montreal Baseball Club, the Montreal Chess Club.

The club-house is on the corner of Mansfield and Berthelet Streets. It contains, besides the gymnasium, reading, bowling, shooting and billiard-rooms, offices and a number of committee and other apartments.

**The St. George's Snowshoe Club** is also a large affair. Its house is on the hillside at Cote St. Antoine. The membership originally consisted principally of Englishmen, whence the name St. George's. This club, like the M.A.A.A., has tramps and dances in winter, and is very popular.

**Le Trappeur** is the principal French Snowshoe Club.

Its costume is blue and white. The club rooms are on St. Lawrence Street, at the corner of Craig.

**The Victoria Skating Rink,** on Drummond Street, is an old institution, with history and prestige, a very large skating hall, and fame for fancy dress carnivals.

A number of other athletic clubs exist, but are more subject to change than the foregoing.

**The Montreal Hunt Club's** elegant "Kennels," on the Papineau Road, are the *locale* of very favourite balls. The pack is an old one, which has been improved upon from the foundation of the club in 1826. The fox-hunting of the club is done in the country districts of the island immediately surrounding the city, and their "breakfasts" at the table of some friend or member are "*récherché* affairs." They also hold steeplechases and other races every year.

Canoeing, boating and yachting are much in vogue, though usually carried on in the watering-places which surround the island, such as Lachine, Dorval, Valois, Pte. Claire, Ste. Anne, Longueuil, Laprairie and Ste. Rose. The Lachine, Valois and Ste. Anne Boat Clubs' club-houses are the chief centres of such amusements. Regattas are held at these places and others during the season.

*Theatres.*

The principal Theatres are: The Academy of Music, Victoria Street; the Queen's Theatre, St. Catherine Street, near English Cathedral; the Theatre Royal, Coté Street. Sohmer Park, on Notre Dame Street East, is a "garden" where musical and French variety performances are given.

*Clubs.*

**St. James' Club,** Dorchester Street West, established in 1857, is the leading social club. It has 460 members and a finely-appointed club-house.

**The Metropolitan Club,** on Beaver Hall Hill, is a flourishing resort of younger men.

**The City Club** is the down-town dining-place of many business men.

**The St. Denis Club,** St. Denis Street, is the leading French Club.

The M.A.A.A. and Y.M.C.A. club-houses serve most of the purposes of social clubs to their members.

# MONTREAL FIFTY YEARS AGO.

Imprinted from a rare collection of original woodblocks now in the possession of Mr. H. T. Martin.

MONTREAL FROM COTE DES NEIGES HILL.

MONKLANDS.

PLACE D'ARMES.

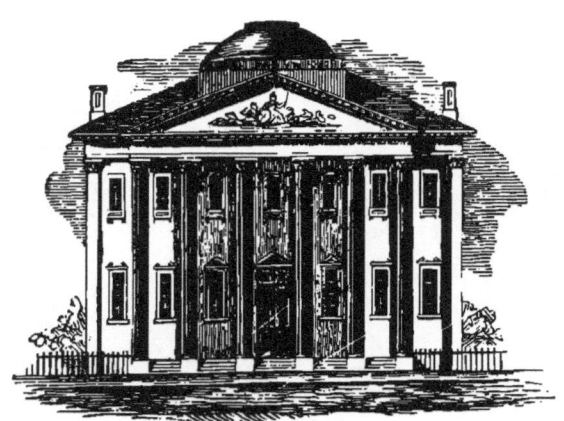

BANK OF MONTREAL.
(With the Dome.)

THE (IMPERIAL) CUSTOM HOUSE TILL 1830.
(South cor. Notre Dame and St. Gabriel Streets.)

OLD ST. GEORGE'S CHURCH.
(St. Joseph Street.)

# HISTORICAL AND LEGENDARY.

# HISTORICAL AND LEGENDARY.

### ABORIGINAL NAME OF THE ISLAND.

THE Savages name it, wrote Père Vimont in the Jesuit *Rélation* for 1642, **Minitik 8ten Entag8giban**—" Isle where there was a town."

### THE DEMONS.

What a delightful sample of mediæval fancy—that these asphalted, crowded, too-civilized streets were once the veritable haunts of imps and Lucifers! On the 15th of August, 1642, the colonists solemnized "the first Festival of this Holy Isle."

"The thunder of the cannon," wrote Père Vimont, "echoed through the entire Island, and the Demons, though accustomed to thunder, were terrified at a sound which spoke of the love we bear to the Great Mistress; I doubt not also that the tutelary Angels of the Savages and of these countries have marked this day in the holidays of Paradise."

## THE ORIGINATORS OF VILLE-MARIE.

The first and calmest originator of the idea of a town here was Champlain. Of a different nature was the visionary Jerôme Le Royer de La Dauversière, who conceived the idea anew a generation later, owing, doubtless, to the fascinating *Rélations* sent home and published throughout France by the Jesuit missionaries. Père Olier, whom some (but not the early historian De Belmont, himself of Olier's own Order) claim to have also separately originated the plan, met him at Meudon at the office of the Keeper of the Seal. "On issuing from the audience with the minister, he met, under the gallery, a man of miserable appearance, who arrived from La Flèche, and waited his turn at the audience. It was a poor collector of taxes, without wealth, without influence, without charm of speech nor of exterior, and whom Providence charged with one of the strangest and most difficult missions for his station: the establishment of a community of hospital nuns to serve a hospital which was non-existent, in a town to be founded, and in a country scarcely even discovered!" "He was accustomed to discipline himself every day, and wore a belt and gloves full of very sharp spikes." Abbé de Belmont relates that before this he had consulted Père La Chaise, who approved the design, and had won to himself the Baron de Faucamp, a rich devotee. Olier joined him at once, gave him 100 louis d'or, and negociated for him a grant of the island from its then proprietor, de Lauzon, a man noted chiefly in the history of Canada for his unblushing and stupendous land-grabs.

**The Company of Nôtre Dame de Montréal,** which they formed, consisted of forty-five persons of quality, including "Madame la Princesse." All the court are said to have contributed. In 1640 they sent over twenty casks of provisions; in 1641, the little colony with their leader Maisonneuve.

There is one thing to be explained away by the friends of de la Dauversière, and which serves to show the weakness of his character. He was the treasurer of the associates; as such, he received, among other sums, one of 12,000 livres of Madame de Bullion's moneys intended for the hospital, which, though he was hopelessly insolvent, he took to pay a private debt of his own, and could never repay.

### THE LANDING-PLACE OF JACQUES CARTIER IN 1535.

The exact locality is disputed. Mr. Gerald Hart, no mean authority, contends that it was at the foot of the Lachine Rapids. It is generally, however, held to be be at the foot of St. Mary's current, where a tablet is being erected concerning it, at the end of Dezéry Street.

As a point in determining the spot, I suggest that it is not likely the Indians would have crossed a stream (the Little River) to get from their town to the St. Lawrence, as they would have had to do had the "broad road" by which Cartier passed to it led from the Rapids.

### SECOND VISIT OF JACQUES CARTIER, 1540.

The object of this visit was to learn about the country beyond the Rapids. Cartier left his fort near Quebec on the 7th of September. On the 11th he arrived at "the first Rapid, which is two leagues from the Town of *Tutonaguy*." Was this another term for Hochelaga? My conjecture is that Tutonaguy was the name of its *Agouhanna*, or "Lord and King of the Country;" and that "the first Rapid" was the St. Mary's current. In any case, the passage throws light on Indian life on the island:

"And after we arrived at that locality, we took counsel to go as far as possible with one of the boats, and that the other should remain there till our return; so we doubled the men in the boat so as to beat against the current of the said rapid. And after we had got far from our other boat, we found bad bottom and large rocks, and so great a current of water that it was not possible to pass beyond with our boat. Whereupon the captain concluded to go by land to see the nature and force of the said Rapid. And after landing, we found near the shore *a road and beaten path* leading to the *said Rapids*. And proceeding, we shortly after found *the dwelling of a tribe* who welcomed us and received us with much friendship. And after we told them we went to the Rapids, and wished to go to Saguenay, four young people come with us to show us the way, and led us so far that we came to another village or dwelling of good people, who live opposite the second Rapid." Then follows some lame geographical palaver. Returning to their boats, they found about 400 people, who seemed very joyous at their arrival. Cartier, however, was then in bad odor with the Indians, and while distributing presents to these people, kept his guard, and at once went back down the river.

## THE FOUNDING OF THE CITY.

The colonists left la Rochelle in two little vessels in the spring of 1641. On the first was de Maisonneuve and 25 men; Mlle. Mance, Père Laplace and 12 men on the other. The latter reached Quebec first. Furious storms drove Maisonneuve's vessel three times back. At last, on the 24th of August, he arrived. The Governor, de Montmagny, and the old colonists desired greatly to keep them at Quebec for the mutual protection, there being only some 200 French in all in the country, and de Montmagny proposed to them the Isle of Orleans near by. "What you propose," replied de Maisonneuve, "would be well had I been sent to consider and choose a post: but the company who send me having fixed that I shall go to Montreal, my honour is concerned, and I shall go up to begin a colony, though all the trees in that island should change into so many Iroquois!" Hence, de Montmagny, with Vimont, Superior of the Jesuits, and some others, went up, and on the 15th of October "fulfilled on the spot the ceremonies prescribed for such things, and took possession of the island in the name of the Company of Montreal."

On the 8th of May, 1642, a little fleet of two barks, a pinnace and a gabare left their resting-places near Quebec, and nine days later, on the 18th of May, the ultimate landing at Montreal took place.

On the 19th of May the woodwork of the Fort was raised. The cannon were placed upon it. Twelve men had been brought, among whom were Minime, the carpenter. The Iroquois, the first year, were quite ignorant of the existence of the Fort. In 1643, ten

Algonquins, having killed an Iroquois in their country, were pursued by the river up to the Fort. The Iroquois then reconnoitred it. This was the precursor of those fierce and incessant attacks which made Montreal the Siege Perilous of early America. The narratives of these encounters had frequently some marvel added by popular story, such as:

THE LEGEND OF THE MIRACULOUS HANDKERCHIEF
OF PÈRE LE MAISTRE.

Père Le Maistre, a devout priest under Olier, came out to the Seminary at Montreal. On the 29th of August, 1661, he accompanied the harvesters into the fields of Fort St. Gabriel, a little fortified farm enclosure now within the edge of the city, where he constituted himself the guard, reciting meanwhile his breviary. He passed so near some Iroquois lying concealed in the brushwood that they, believing themselves discovered, sprang upon him with fierce war cries. Careless of peril to himself, he called out to his men to run. The savages, seeing their prey escaping, took revenge upon him, cut off his head, and carried it off in a handkerchief. But his features, say the accounts of the time, remained imprinted thereon. "What is peculiar," they write, "is that there was no blood on the handkerchief, and that it was very white. It appeared on the upper side like a very fine white wax, which bore the face of the servant of God." They say even that it spoke to them at times and reproached them for their cruelty, and that, in order to free themselves of this oracle which

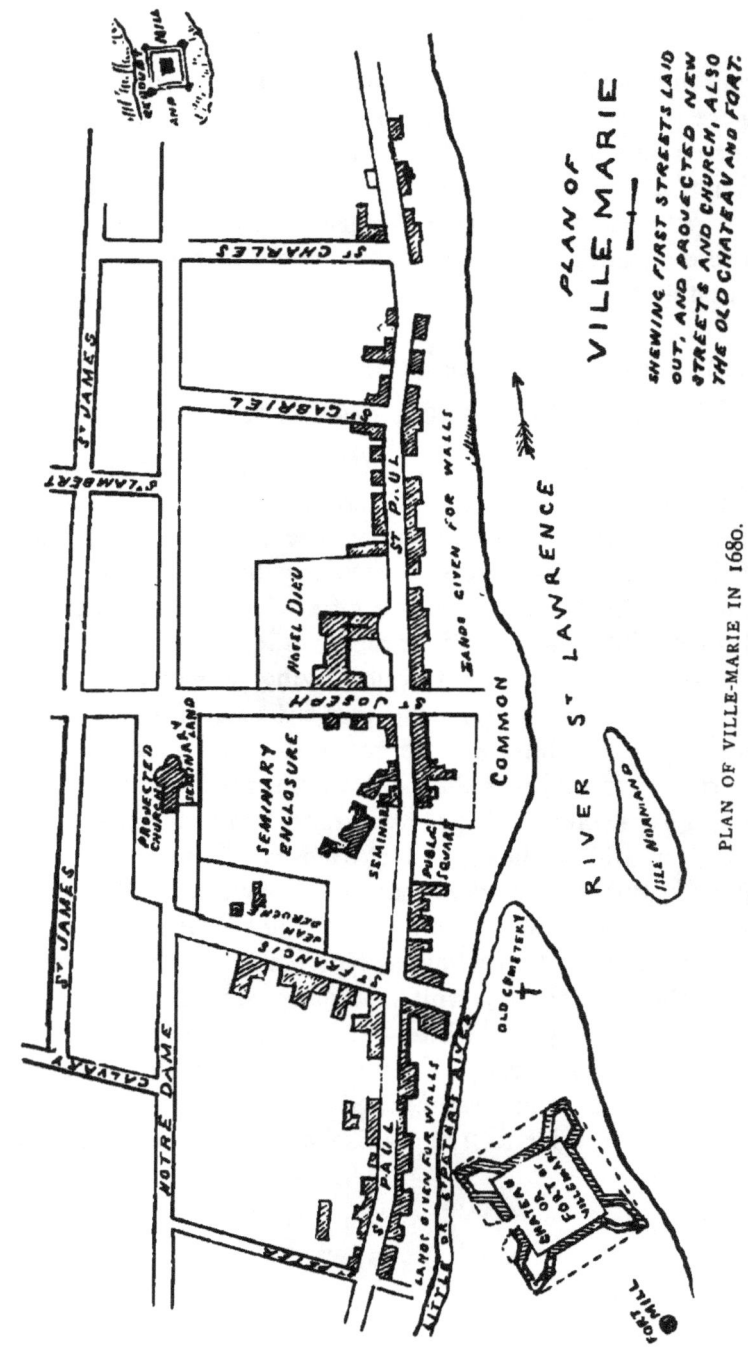

PLAN OF VILLE-MARIE IN 1680.

terrified them, they sold the handkerchief to the English. Hoondoroen, the murderer, became converted, and died at the mission of St. Sulpice."

### THE HEAD OF JEAN SAINT PÈRE.

"In the autumn of 1657 there was a truce with the Iroquois, under cover of which three or four of them came to the settlement. Nicolas Godé and Jean St. Père (notary royal) were on the roof of their house, laying thatch, when one of the visitors aimed his arquebuse at St. Père and brought him to the ground. Now ensued a prodigy, for the assassins, having cut off his head and carried it home to their village, were amazed to hear it speak to them in good Iroquois, scold them for their perfidy and threaten them with the vengeance of Heaven; and they continued to hear its voice of admonition even after scalping it and throwing away the skull."—*Parkman's Old Régime.*

### THE DEATH OF LAMBERT CLOSSE.

Closse, the brave town major, found, with disappointment, that his various companions were one by one falling from time to time in the Iroquois fighting. "And yet," complained he, "I came to Ville-Marie only to die for God, in serving Him in the profession of arms. Had I known I would not perish so, I should quit this land and serve against the Turks, that I might not lose this glory." God satisfied him on the 6th of February, 1662. Some colonists, working in his fields, being attacked by a band of Iroquois, he ran at once to their defence, according to his custom, and would have saved them except for the cowardice of a Fleming, who deserted him. Closse fell in the encounter, and thus achieved the glory he so often desired.

The place of the combat was somewhere near the corner of Craig Street and St. Lambert Hill (which receives its name from his own). The Antiquarian Society's tablet, erected on the the south corner of St. Lambert Hill and St. James Street, near the site of his house, reads: "Near to this place Raphael Lambert Closse, first Town Major of Ville-Marie, fell bravely defending some colonists attacked by Iroquois, 6th February, 1662. In his honour St. Lambert Hill received its name." The name was given ten years afterwards, showing that his heroism was not easily forgotten.

ANOTHER IROQUOIS FIGHT.

Another of the many stirring deeds of those days is related on a tablet on the corner of Campeau and Lagauchetiere Streets: "Here Trudeau, Roulier and Langevin-Lacroix resisted 50 Iroquois."

The incident took place in 1662. "The sixth of May," writes Dollier de Casson, the blood of the soldier stirring under his cassock, "a fine fight was made at Ste. Marie. The Seminary had established the post of that name at the lower end of the settlement, in the same way as St. Gabriel above. It was opposite the little rapid down the harbour, still known as St. Mary's Current, and was placed among some fifty acres which had been cleared and cultivated, in prehistoric days, by the Indians. The three men were returning to the habitation after their day's work in the fields, when one of them suddenly cried: "To arms, the enemy are upon us!" At the same moment a large party of Iroquois, who had been lurking near by all day, rose and fired. Each Frenchman seized his musket and fled to a hole near by, called "the Redoubt." This they held stoutly till rescued by DeBelestre, commandant at Ste. Marie, and after a brisk fight, the enemy finally retired to the woods.

### DOLLARD DES ORMEAUX.

But the grand legend of Ville-Marie is the Story of Dollard. A little old French street, now used as a lane, off St. James Street, bears his name to-day, and the tablet on it, near the latter street, runs: "To Adam Dollard des Ormeaux, who, with 16 colonists, 4 Algonquins and 1 Huron, sacrificed their lives at the Long Sault of the Ottawa, 21st May, 1660, and saved the Colony."

The narrative in the "Jesuit Relations" is somewhat as follows: Forty of the sad remnant of the once-great Hurons—destroyed by the merciless warfare of the Iroquois, "who only breathe the air of war"—led by a chief of renown named Anahotaha, left Quebec in the spring of 1660 on the warpath. At Three Rivers, six Algonquins joined them, under the chief Miti8emeg. At Montreal they found that seventeen French had already united with the same design, generously sacrificing themselves for the public good and the defence of religion. They had chosen for their chief the Sieur Dollard, who, though only lately arrived from France, was found the right man for this kind of war, and eager to take part in it. He is said to have been an army officer in France, and to have committed an offence, which he was anxious to wash away by some heroic sacrifice. They all shrived themselves solemnly in the Parish Church, and set out together with courage.

They marched by night, and dragged their canoes through the icy waters and remnants of snow till they came to the foot of "the Long Leap" of the Ottawa River, and posted themselves to await the coming of the Iroquois hunters, who, according to their custom, would pass along in single file returning from their winter hunt. They were no sooner posted than perceived by the Iroquois. A skirmish took place with five of the enemy, and soon afterwards about 200 Onondagas appeared in war-dress descending the rapid in their canoes. The French party, surprised and seeing themselves so feeble in numbers, rushed and took possession of a wretched ruin of a fort erected there by some Algonquins in the autumn. There they entrenched themselves as best they could. The Onondagas crept up and finally attacked with fury. They were repulsed with loss. Despairing of success by force, they had resort to their Indian methods, requesting a parley, but at the same time secretly sending off for the Mohawks. And while on one side of the fort apparently peaceable, they suddenly attacked it on the other; but the French were on their guard. They were for a short time disheartened; but soon after, the Mohawks, estimated at 500, came up with whoops so horrible and loud, that all the region around seemed full of Iroquois. Firing kept up day and night, attacks were sharp and frequent, and the French employed the intervals kneeling in constant prayer. So passed ten days.

Thirst now became pressing, for the river was 200 paces away, and this want caused the Indian allies to send and treat for peace with the enemy. On assurances of life, thirty leaped the palisades and deserted, thus fatally weakening the besieged. Messengers were then sent forward to propose surrender to the latter; but the French for answer fired upon them. This so enraged the Iroquois, that they all rose up, ferociously rushed at the palisade with heads down, and began to sap it with their axes in the face of the heavy fire. The French called up all their courage and industry in this extremity. Among other efforts they took up a keg of powder, lit a fuse to it, and threw it out among the assailants. It unfortunately struck a branch, sprang back into the fort, and exploded, burning most of the defenders and blinding them with its fumes. The Iroquois were so elated, that they sprang furiously over the palisade on all sides, hatchet in hand, and filled it with blood and carnage, killing all but five of the French and four Hurons, among the slain being the brave Anahotaha, who, dying, begged his comrades to thrust his head in the fire, so that no Iroquois should have the glory of taking his scalp. At this moment a Frenchman arose. Seeing that all was lost, and that several of his companions, while fatally wounded, still survived, he finished them with great strokes of an axe, to deliver them from the Iroquois fires. The foe took their revenge by terrible tortures of the living, and by eating their flesh. But the design, before formed in their councils, of overrunning and finally exterminating the French settlement was thenceforward abandoned.

If seventeen French, with but five allies, could fight so well, what might the rest do if pushed to an extremity? The whole colony was thus saved from peril and destruction by the deed of the heroes of the Long Sault.

<blockquote>What though beside the foaming flood untombed their ashes lie,<br>
All earth becomes the monument of men who nobly die.</blockquote>

"The spirit of the enterprise," says Parkman, "was purely mediæval. The enthusiasm of honour, the enthusiasm of adventure and the enthusiasm of faith were its motive forces. Daulac (Dollard) was a knight of the early Crusades among the forests and savages of the New World. Yet the incidents of this exotic heroism are definite and clear as a tale of yesterday. The names, ages and occupations of the seventeen young men may still be read on the ancient register of the Parish of Montreal."

## THE GREAT EARTHQUAKE.

The signs and wonders attributed to the Great Earthquake of 1662, which endured for some six months, and was considered a miraculous time of visitation for the sins of the colony, were such as these:

"For forty days," says a narrator, "we saw from all points of this town men on horseback who rushed through the air richly robed and armed with lances, like troops of cavalry; steeds ranged in squadrons which dashed forth against each other; combatants, who joined battle hand to hand; shields shaken; a multitude armed in helmets and naked swords; wherefore they prayed God to turn these prodigies to their advantage."

Another relates: "Earth and heaven spoke to us many times this year. . . . . Last autumn we saw (in the sky) serpents which entwined themselves into one another and flew through the air bearing wings of fire."

### NAMING OF THE STREETS.

It was the able and genial Dollier de Casson, the first historian of Montreal, who, as Superior of the Seminary, laid out the streets in 1672. Notre Dame Street, drawn through the centre, he named after the patron saint of the community; St. Paul Street, in honour of Paul de Chomédy de Maisonneuve; St. James Street (Rue St. Jacques), of Jacques Olier; St. Peter, of the Baron de Fancamp; St. François, of himself; St. Lambert, of brave Lambert Closse; St. Gabriel, of Abbé Gabriel de Queylus and Abbé Gabriel Souart; and St. Jean Baptiste, of the great French Minister Colbert, whose extensive reforms extended to Canada.

### THE BURNING OF THE FOUR IROQUOIS, 1696.

An eye-witness of the burning of the four Iroquois on what is now Jacques Cartier Square thus describes it: "When I came to Montreal for the first time, it was by the St. Francis Gate. I there saw a man of my province, who came up to embrace me, which he did and after some compliments, informed me that he was of our company. As we were speaking together, he perceived that I was much distracted because of a large crowd that I saw on the Place des Jésuites. Thereupon my new comrade exclaimed: 'Upon my word! you've just come in time to see four Iroquois burnt alive.

Come on as far as the Jésuites; we'll see better.' It was immediately in front of their door that this bloody tragedy was to take place. I thought at first they would throw the poor wretches into a fire; but on looking around on all sides, I saw no faggots for the sacrifice of the victims, and I questioned my new friend about several small fires which I saw at certain distances apart from each other. He answered me: 'Patience; we are going to have some good laughing.' For some, however, it was no laughing matter. They led out these four wild men, who were brothers, and the finest looking men I have ever seen in my life. Then the Jesuits baptised them and made them some scanty exhortations; for, to speak freely, to do more would have been 'to wash the head of a corpse.' The holy ceremony finished, they were taken hold of and submitted to punishments of which they were the inventors. They bound them naked to stakes stuck three or four feet in the ground, and then each of our Indian allies, as well as several Frenchmen, armed themselves with bits of red-hot iron, wherewith they broiled all parts of their bodies. Those small fires which I had seen served as forges to heat the abominable instruments with which they roasted them. Their torture lasted six hours, during which they never ceased to chant of their deeds of war, while drinking brandy, which passed down their throats as quickly as if it had been thrown into a hole in the ground. Thus died these unfortunates with an inexpressible constancy and courage. I was told that what I saw was but a feeble sample of what they make us suffer when they take us prisoners."

## DWELLING-PLACES OF CELEBRITIES, ETC.

### La Salle.

On a building at the corner of St. Peter and St. Paul Streets is seen the inscription: "Here lived Robert Cavelier, Sieur de La Salle, 1668."

La Salle, one of the most attractive and chivalrous characters of those days, was born in 1643, of a rich and ancient merchant family of Rouen; was with the Jesuits in his youth; in 1666, came out to Montreal, where he had a brother, Abbé Jean Cavelier, a priest of St. Sulpice. Ville-Marie, the Castle Dangerous of the time, no doubt attracted his adventurous nature. The Seminary soon offered to him the grant of a seigniory of wild lands at Lachine, where he began to found a settlement, laying out a palisaded village. Hearing, however, of the Mississippi, his imagination took fire, and he threw himself into the project of following it to its mouth, which, he contended, must lead into the Gulf of Mexico. Frontenac encouraged him, the Seminary bought out his improvements. He built Fort Frontenac on the site of Kingston. He went to France, where the court favoured his projects. In 1679, he embarked on Lake Erie. He reached the Mississippi in 1682, followed its course to the Gulf of Mexico, returned to France, and sailed thence direct to Louisiana, where he perished by assassination in the wilds by two mutineers among his men in 1687. Parkman's "La Salle and the Discovery of the Great West" relates at length the brilliant story of his discoveries.

The house upon the site of which the tablet is placed

has long since disappeared. It was leased by him on the 15th of November, 1668, from Sieur Rabutel de St. André, a comparatively wealthy proprietor of houses.

### Du Luth.

On the Place d'Armes, at the street corner nearest the Parish Church, is a tablet reading; "In 1675, here lived Daniel de Grésolon, Sieur Dulhut, one of the explorers of the Upper Mississippi; after whom the City of Duluth was named."

Dulhut, or Du Luth, was a masterly man. In France he was in the army as a gentleman soldier—Gendarme of the King's Guard. In 1677, he left the army, and coming to Canada, went among the Sioux of the West as a rover, remaining about three years, solely exploring.

He was then appointed commander of posts in the West, including Detroit, until recalled to Montreal in 1688. Some say he then built the first fortifications of Montreal—of palisades. Next year, during the panic which followed the Iroquois invasion of Montreal, he, with 28 Canadians, attacked 22 Iroquois in canoes, on the Lake of Two Mountains, received their fire without returning it, bore down upon them, killed 18 of them and captured 3. He died about 1710.

### La Mothe Cadillac.

Tablet on Notre Dame Street, just east of St. Lambert Hill: "In 1694, here stood the house of La Mothe Cadillac, the founder of Detroit."

Cadillac was an able man, but bore a bad reputation. He commanded at Detroit, and is generally called its founder; but a fort was built near the present city before his time. His wife superintended his warehouse here, and sold his merchandise as it came from the West.

### D'Aillebout de Coulonge.

The tablet sufficiently explains this name: "Chevalier Louis d'Ailleboust de Coulonge, one of the chief defenders of Ville-Marie, of which he was Governor, 1645–1647. Fourth Governor of New France, 1648–1651. Died 31 May, 1660." (Place of erection not yet decided, but to be somewhere near the Custom House.)

His arrival with a small force of soldiers, and his personal courage, were a great assistance to Maisonneuve.

### Charles LeMoyne—Iberville—Bienville.

For J. G. Mackenzie & Co.'s store, St. Paul Street, just east of Custom House Square, are proposed three tablets. The first is: "Here was the residence of Charles LeMoyne, one of the companions of Maisonneuve. Among his children, Charles, first Baron of Longueuil; Jacques, Sieur de Ste. Hélène; Pierre, Sieur d'Iberville; Paul, Sieur de Maricour; François, Sieur de Bienville I.; Joseph, Sieur de Serigny; François Marie, Sieur de Sauvalle; Jean Baptiste, Sieur de Bienville II.; Gabriel, Sieur d'Assigny; Antoine, Sieur de Châteauguay; rendered the colony illustrious."

Charles LeMoyne, subject of this rather long inscription, right-hand man of de Maisonneuve, and father of sons celebrated in the annals of New France, was the son of an innkeeper of Dieppe, but withal a most fearless and intelligent man. He came from France a youth only fifteen, was sent among the Indians forthwith to be an interpreter, and caught the spirit of warlike forest life. He several times saved Ville-Marie from Indian attacks, at one time just saving the Hotel Dieu. At another he walked coolly down to a war-party of Iroquois and marched them up to the fort at the point of his pistols. Point St. Charles is named from him, his farm having extended thither along the shore. About fourteen years after Ville-Marie was founded, he was given the seigniory of Longueuil opposite, which he proceeded to settle, fortify and develop in an able manner. Through this source, with the fur trade and the furnishing of public supplies, he amassed comparative wealth. His cousin and partner, LeBer, became the richest merchant of the country.

LeMoyne's eldest son became Baron of Longueuil, having built there, in 1699, a fine feudal castle, which existed till the end of last century.

The tablets to D'Iberville and Bienville need no comment. They are as follows: "Here was born, in 1661, Pierre LeMoyne, Sieur d'Iberville, Chevalier de St. Louis. He conquered Hudson's Bay for France, 1697; discovered the mouths of the Mississippi, 1699. First Governor of Louisiana, 1700. Died at Havana, 1706."

"Jean Baptiste LeMoyne, Sieur de Bienville; born in 1680. In company with his brother, d'Iberville, he discovered the mouths of the Mississippi, 2 March, 1699; founded New Orleans in 1717; and was Governor of Louisiana for forty years. Died at Paris, 1768."

### The First Schoolmaster.

On the corner of Notre Dame and St. Sulpice Streets: "Here M. de LaPrairie opened the first private school in Montreal, 1683." This is the same property which Du Luth at one time leased and occupied.

### The De Catalogne House.

In a neighbourhood of old houses, on St. Vincent Street, adjoining Rickett's Saloon, is a long dwelling of two stories and attic, well-preserved and strong. This was the home built for himself by the Engineer of the first Lachine Canal, and the one first concerned in the plans of the earliest stone fortification walls.

On the 30th of October, 1700, Dollier de Casson, for the Seminary, passed an agreement with de Catalogne, therein described as "officer in the Marines and Royal Surveyor," whereby the latter was to excavate a canal from the Grand or St. Lawrence River to the River St. Pierre. The cut was to be twelve French feet wide and nine deep, the length some 800 yards, the price 3,000 livres (francs), and the time of completion June, 1701. It was the first canal contract in Canada. The canal was begun, but never completed, the amount of rock to be excavated constituting the final difficulty. As far as de Catalogne is concerned, he claimed the death of de Casson, which happened in October, 1701, to have been the cause, and that his death cost the former 3,000 *écus*. The tablet inscription reads: "1693. House of Gédéon de Catalogne, engineer, officer and chronicler. Projector of the earliest Lachine Canal."

The house stands a kind of monument of the skill of its owner and builder. The notes of contemporary fighting and events written by him are clear-headed, frank and just. He served on several expeditions, and was in some severe fighting, notably the Battle of Laprairie. The cut made for his canal at Lachine can yet be seen near the head of the present canal.

### *The Tomb of Kondiaronk (The Rat.)*

On the 3rd of August, 1701, this wily, able Huron chief, a noted figure in the early savage days, was buried in the Old Parish Church. It consequently seems to follow that his remains still lie under Notre Dame Street, in front of the Parish Church. He was a friend of the French, but prevented them, by a singular network of adroit perfidy, from making peace with his enemies, the Iroquois. Murdering some of the latter just when a peace treaty was being proposed, he led their tribes to believe it the work of the French, at the same time similarly misreporting the Iroquois to the colonists. He died just following a harangue to the allied tribes assembled at Montreal. On his tomb were inscribed the words: " Here lies Le Rat, the Huron Chief."

### *Vaudreuil—Montcalm—Lévis.*

On Jacques Cartier Square, where St. Paul Street crosses it, stood the great mansion and gardens of the Marquis de Vaudreuil, last French Governor of Canada, as the tablet mentioned in describing the square records. It was erected on the site of the large house built and occupied by Du Luth in his latter days. The Marquis, son of the first Governor-General of the same name and title, was born a Canadian, a fact which led Montcalm and Lévis, the successive commanders-in-chief of the French army, to underrate him; but he, as a man of local knowledge and calm judgment, was their superior. The place has memories of them also, since, as his official guests, they resided here for considerable periods. The death of Montcalm at the loss of Quebec gives an undying tragic interest to any spot connected with him. Fancy pictures upon this square the château and great garden of those days, the silken Louis XIV. costumes of the beaux and dames, the powdered wigs, the high Pompadour head-dresses, the hurrying lackeys, the French guard of honour in their spotless blue and white uniform, and, centre of all observation, the melancholy and stately but courteous young hero, Louis Joseph, Marquis de Montcalm-Gozon, the hope of all hearts except his own.

On St. Helen's Island, a tablet is placed which concerns Lévis more particularly. It relates his withdrawal to that position and his burning his flags by night. A tradition states that he signed the capitulation of the city against a tree near the head of the Island.

## La Vérandrye.

Pierre Gauthier de Varennes, Sieur de la Vérandrye, whose father was the struggling seigneur of a forest seigniory just below Longueuil, was the discoverer of the Rocky Mountains (1742), and was the first trader to explore the North-West proper. First he entered the French Army in the campaigns in Flanders, where he had a brother an officer. At the Battle of Malplaquet, he distinguished himself by such bravery, that, after being left for dead upon the field, covered with sabre-cuts, he was made a lieutenant. He returned to Canada, and soon conceived the project of pushing through to the Pacific across the continent. This he followed out for many years (1731-48), with scant support, establishing post after post, at Rainy Lake, Lake of the Woods, Lake Winnipeg, and on the Saskatchewan itself, and losing his son by Indian murder in the West. He gave a great region to France, and, through her, to Canada, but was never properly requited, though the Marquis de la Jonquière made him in the end captain of his guard at Quebec. He died in 1749.

### *Palace of the Intendant.*

This stood upon the same site afterwards occupied by the house of Sir John Johnson, where the west half of the Bonsecours Market is. It was originally the mansion of the Barons of Longueuil, erected in 1698, and was removed in 1793. The Intendant was the chief officer in the colony in its civil administration, as the governor was in its military. Hence rivalry and sometimes conflicts of jurisdiction between these offices. This palace was the headquarters in Montreal of the infamous Intendant Bigot, who, by his profligacy and régime of dishonest extravagance, ruined the resources of the colony and hastened its fall. A good picture of the characters of his circle is given by William Kirby in his novel, " The Chien d'Or," published by John Lovell & Son, Montreal.

### La Friponne.

This old stone building, yet standing, on the corner of Friponne Street, near Dalhousie Square, was the French Government warehouse, in which many of the frauds of Intendant Bigot and his comrades, upon both the government and the people, were carried on. The principal warehouse was at Quebec, and also was known by the name of the *Friponne*, which means the Swindle.

### Près-de-Ville.

This house, a wing of the present Christian Brothers' School, Coté Street, cannot be well seen without entering the grounds. It has been greatly altered and raised, and part of it at one time burnt; but a bastioned wing still stands out on a quaint boulder foundation in a manner which makes it one of the most interesting-looking of our buildings. It was the house of LeMoyne de Maricour, one of the family of brothers celebrated in the early military enterprises of the colony, and including Bienville, Iberville and the first Baron of Longueuil.

### The De Beaujeu House.

This is on St. Antoine Street, corner of St. Margaret, and is to bear the following inscription in French: "Here lived the family of Daniel Hyacinthe Marie Liénard de Beaujeu, the Hero of the Monongahela; at which battle Washington was an officer in the army defeated."

The Battle of the Monongahela River in Ohio was the occasion of the slaughter of a fine army of three thousand men through the incredible vanity of General

Braddock, an officer who had earned a European reputation for courage, but who, despising the advice of the provincial officers, insisted on his men fighting in the forest with the same columns and tactics as on the open field. The result was lamentable, and to the great surprise of the French commander, he was enabled to rout the large and finely equipped force. They were saved by the provincials, who took to their forest methods, and at length, under Washington, patched up a truce, and thus rescued the remnants of the English regiments of the expedition. De Beaujeu died of his wounds shortly after.

*The British Conquest, 1760.—Amherst, Murray, Haviland.*

This imposing event, when the vast Empire of France in America passed away, identified with Montreal a number of distinguished men. A world-wide lustre rested upon the brilliant circle of "the Heroes of Quebec," many of whom remained for longer or shorter periods. Such were Generals Murray, Gage, Burton, Carleton and "Lord Amherst of Montreal."

After the battle of the Plains of Abraham, where Wolfe and Montcalm fell and Quebec was lost, it became evident that the province could not hold out much longer. General Lévis retired with the French army up the river towards Montreal, returning once only to make an attempt on Quebec. The British the next summer completed arrangements for marching upon him from three directions—one, down the St. Lawrence from Oswego, under Sir Jeffery Amherst, with

10,000 men; a second under Colonel Haviland, with 3,400, by way of Lake Champlain; and the third under General Murray, with 3,780, up the river from Quebec. The three armies were to converge towards Montreal. So efficiently was all planned and carried out, that they arrived from their respective directions within a very few hours of each other. Amherst came first, passing all the rapids safely, and reaching Lachine on the 6th of September, whence he pushed on quickly, and that night "occupied the heights" by taking possession of Côte des Neiges Hill, looking towards the city. The position of his camp-ground is remembered traditionally, and is marked by an inscription on the front walls of the Collège de Montreal Grounds, Sherbrooke Street West, in these words: "This tablet is erected to commemorate the encampment, near this spot, of the British Army under Major-General Sir Jeffery Amherst, and the closing event in the conquest of Cape Breton and Canada by the surrender of Montreal, and with it La Nouvelle France, 8 September, 1760."

On the hill above may be seen from the high road the ruins of a stone cottage, situated in a market-garden. According to tradition, Amherst had made this his headquarters, and one of the tablets marks it thus: "Tradition asserts that the Capitulation of Montreal and Canada was signed here, 1760."

Next morning, Murray landed below the city, and marching up, encamped in line with Amherst, further east on the Sherbrooke Street terrace, about where, at the corner of Park Avenue, a tablet is placed, reading: "Major-General James Murray, Brigade Commander under Wolfe at Quebec, 1759, and afterwards first British Governor of Canada, encamped on this plateau with the second division of Amherst's army, upon the surrender of Montreal and all Canada, 8 September, 1760."

Haviland meanwhile appeared simultaneously across the river at Longueuil.

The defences of the town were that useless mound called the Citadel, and the somewhat imposing-looking, but thin and weak, stone walls, useful in their time against Indians, but not for an hour against cannon. The Canadians were discouraged; the army reduced by desertion to about 4,000 dispirited regulars. There was, therefore, no alternative but to surrender, and Governor Vaudreuil drew up, in fifty-five articles of capitulation, the best terms he could. Nearly all were accepted by Amherst, but he emphatically refused the troops their arms and the honours of war. "The whole garrison," he declared, "must lay down their arms." The French found this hard, and remonstrated. Amherst answered that it was to mark his abhorrence of the barbarities permitted by them to their savage allies during the preceding events of the war—alluding, clearly, to the massacre of prisoners at Fort William Henry under the very eyes of Lévis some years before. The morning of the 8th of September, Vaudreuil signed the capitulation. It was then that Lévis secretly burnt his flags on St. Helen's Island to avoid surrendering them. He, however, gave his word of honour to Amherst that they had been previously lost. The character of Vaudreuil contrasts favourably with that of Lévis in the whole of these transactions. A tradition asserts that the keys of the city were given over by a woman.

On the evening of the 8th, a British force, commanded by Colonel Haldimand, afterwards Governor, entered the Récollet Gate by arrangement, and took possession of the Récollet Quarter, which was then largely open space, chiefly covered by the gardens of the monastery. The French withdrew to their camp by the citadel at the other end of the town. On the 9th, the Journal of Lévis records: "They (the British) sent a detachment upon the Place d'Armes with artillery, whither our battalions marched to lay down their arms, one after the other, and return to the camp they occupied on the rampart. M. le Chevalier de Lévis then reviewed them. The enemy took possession of the posts and all the watches of the city."

A few days later, what was left of the troops of France embarked, with their chiefs, on the way home.

### Gage.

Among the other interesting men whom the invasion brought to Montreal, was the one to whom the tablet on the Dalhousie Square Fire Station, next the old military headquarters, is erected, with the words: "To Brigadier-General Thomas Gage, second in command under Amherst; first British Governor of Montreal, 1760; afterwards last British Governor of Massachusetts. 1775."

He it was who kept New York City a British stronghold all through the Revolution.

K

### Sir William Johnson.

A tablet relating to another well-known man in colonial history stands upon the Bonsecours Market, where was the residence of his son. It reads: "Sir William Johnson, of Johnson Hall on the Mohawk River, the celebrated Superintendent of Indian Affairs, and first American Baronet, commanded the Indian allies with Amherst's army in 1760. To them was issued, in commemoration, the first British Montreal medal. Here stood the house of his son, Sir John Johnson, Indian Commissioner."

### Burton.

The house where this Hero of Quebec long resided stood on St. Paul Street, opposite the Bonsecours Market. His daughter married General Christie (the second Commander-in-chief of the Forces in Canada of that name), who added the name of Burton to his own. A fine portrait of Burton is in the Art Gallery. The inscription for the site of his residence is: "Site of the house of General Ralph Burton, second Governor of Montreal, 1763. He executed, on the Plains of Abraham, at Wolfe's dying command, the military operation which finally decided the day."

The reference is to Wolfe's last words: "'Who run?' Wolfe demanded, like a man roused from sleep. 'The enemy, sir. Egad they give way everywhere!' 'Go one of you to Colonel Burton,' returned the dying man; 'tell him to march Webb's regiment down to Charles River, to cut off their retreat from the Bridge.' Then turning on his side, he murmured: 'Now, God be praised, I will die in peace!'"*

It might also have been added that Burton was distinguished for courage in the disastrous blunder of the Monongahela.

### The North-Westers.

The North-West Fur Company's stores, around which so much history in adventure, discovery and commerce centres, are on St. Gabriel Street, opposite the Fire Station, near Notre Dame Street. Hither came Sir Alexander Mackenzie and Simon Fraser (the discoverer), Alexander Henry, John Jacob Astor, Washington Irving, McTavish, Franchère, the Highland laird, the English general, the Indian brave.

The tall, peaked warehouse, neatly built of stone and protected by iron shutters, which faces one looking through the gateway, carries the date "1793," surrounded by four stars. The company was an association composed of the principal Scottish and French-Canadian merchants, who had replaced the French traders to the West. As, by their activity, system and enterprise, they greatly improved their business and extended its territory, they both became wealthy local men of their time, and also the rivals of the older Hudson's Bay Company. The newer association was organized in 1783. "The sleepy old Hudson's Bay Company," says one writer, "were astounded at the magnificence of the new-comers, and old traders yet talk of the lordly Nor'-Wester. It was in those days that Washington Irving

---

* Parkman's "Montcalm and Wolfe."

was their guest when he made his memorial journey to Montreal. The agents who presided at headquarters were veterans that had grown grey in the wilds, and were full of all the traditions of the fur trade ; and around them circled the laurels gained in the North."

"To behold the North-West Company in all its state and grandeur," writes Irving himself in *Astoria*, "it was necessary to witness the annual gathering at Fort William, near what is now called the Grand Portage, on Lake Superior. On these occasions might be seen the change since the unceremonious times of the old French traders, with their roystering *coureurs de bois*. Now the aristocratic character of the Briton, or rather the feudal spirit of the Highlander, shone out magnificently; every partner who had charge of an interior post, and had a score of retainers at his command, felt like the chieftain of a Highland clan. To him, a visit to the grand conference at Fort William was a most important event, and he repaired thither as to a meeting of Parliament. The partners from Montreal were, however, the lords of the ascendant. They ascended the rivers in great state, like sovereigns making a progress. They were wrapped in rich furs, their huge canoes freighted with every convenience and luxury. Fort William, the scene of this important meeting, was a considerable village on the banks of Lake Superior. Here, in an immense wooden building, was the great council-chamber, and also the banqueting-hall, decorated with Indian arms and accoutrements and the trophies of the fur trade. The great and weighty councils were alternated with huge feasts and revels."

## Alexander Henry.

On a house near the foot of St. Urbain Street, on the west side, are the words : " Here lived, 1760-1824, Alexander Henry, the Traveller, Author and Fur-Trader."

Henry was the pioneer of the English fur-trade in the West. He had a thrilling escape from massacre during the well-known capture of Fort Michillimackinac, by the French Indian Pontiac, effected by means of a game of lacrosse, in 1763. Parkman gives an account of his escape in "The Conspiracy of Pontiac," but Henry's own book, "Travels and Adventures in Canada and the Indian Territories," dated from Montreal, and published in 1809, is a well-written narrative of all his adventures. His discoveries extended far to the North, and enabled him to obtain from northern Indians some information of the streams which flow into the Arctic Ocean.

## Mackenzie.

On the premises of Wm. Smith, Esq., near the head of Simpson Street, is a tablet of great interest: " Site of the residence of Sir Alexander Mackenzie, discoverer of the Mackenzie River, 1793, and the first European to cross the Rocky Mountains."

For five years, from about 1779, he was in the counting-house of Mr. Gregory, a Montreal merchant, but then went to the North-West Company's Fort Chippewyan on Lake Arthabasca, whence he started on the two momentous expeditions referred to in the tablet. In the first, he travelled a thousand miles northward along the great river of his name, until he neared the Arctic Ocean, In the second, he reached the Pacific.

### *Fraser.*

The tablet to the British Columbia explorer reads: " To Simon Fraser, Agent of the North-West Company, discoverer of the Fraser River, 1808."

This energetic Nor'-Wester is spoken of as a man of stern and repellant manner. He died at St. Andrews', Glengarry, Ontario.

### *Brant—Tecumseh.*

These chiefs were both here—the first, at a great Indian council held by the Johnsons at Montreal, in the summer of 1775 ; the latter, during the war of 1812. A tablet recording his visit is being drawn for erection.

### MONTREAL IN 1666.

"Approaching the shore where the city of Montreal now stands, one would have seen a row of small, compact dwellings, extending along a narrow street parallel to the river, and then, as now, called St. Paul Street. On a hill at the right stood the windmill of the seigneurs, built of stone and pierced with loopholes to serve, in time of need, as a place of defence. On the left, in an angle formed by the junction of a rivulet with the St. Lawrence, was a bastioned fort of stone. Here lived the military governor, appointed by the Seminary, and commanding a few soldiers of the regiment of Carignan. In front, on the line of the street, were the enclosures of the Seminary, and nearly adjoining them, those of the

Hotel Dieu or Hospital, both provided for defence in case of an Indian attack. In the Hospital enclosure was a small church, opening on the street, and, in the absence of any other, serving for the whole settlement."

So writes Parkman. The account, though incorrect in a couple of trifling particulars, is accurate as a general picture.

### THE CITY IN 1770.

The following is from Wynne's "General History of the British Empire in America," 1770—a title which of itself is food for thought:

"Montreal, situated on the island of that name, the second place in Canada for extent, buildings and strength, besides possessing the advantages of a less rigorous climate, for delightfulness of situation is infinitely preferable to Quebec. It stands on the side of a hill sloping down to the river, with the south country and many gentlemen's seats thereon, together with the island of St. Helen, all in front, which form a charming landscape, the River St. Lawrence here being about two miles across. Though the city is not very broad from north to south, it covers a great length of ground from east to west, and is nearly as large and populous as Quebec.

"The streets are regular, forming an oblong square, the houses well built, and in particular the public buildings, which far exceed those of the capital in beauty and commodiousness, the residence of the Knights Hospitallers (?) being extremely magnificent. There are several gardens within the walls, in which, however, the proprietors have consulted use more than elegance, particularly those of the Sisters of the Congregation, the Nunnery Hospital, the Récollets, Jesuits, Seminary and Governor. Besides these, there are many other gardens and beautiful plantations without the gates, as the garden of the General Hospital, and the improvements of Mr. Liniere, which exceed all the rest, and are at an agreeable distance on the north side of the town. The three churches and religious houses are plain, and contain no paintings nor anything remarkable or curious, but carry the appearance of the utmost neatness and simplicity.

" The city has six or seven gates, large and small, but its fortifications are mean and inconsiderable, being encompassed by a slight wall of masonry, fully calculated to awe the numerous tribes of Indians, who resorted here at all times from the most distant parts for the sake of traffic, particularly at the fair held here every year, which continued from the beginning of June till the latter end of August, when many solemnities were observed ; and the Governor assisted and guards were placed to preserve good order in such a concourse of so great a variety of savage nations. There are no batteries on the walls except for flank-fires, and most of these are binded with planks and loop-holes, made at the embrasures for musketry. Some writers have represented these walls to be four feet in thickness, but they are mistaken. They are built of stone, the parapet of the curtains does not exceed twenty inches, and the mertins at the flank-fires are somewhat thicker, though not near three feet. A dry ditch surrounds this wall about seven feet deep, encompassed with a regular glacis.

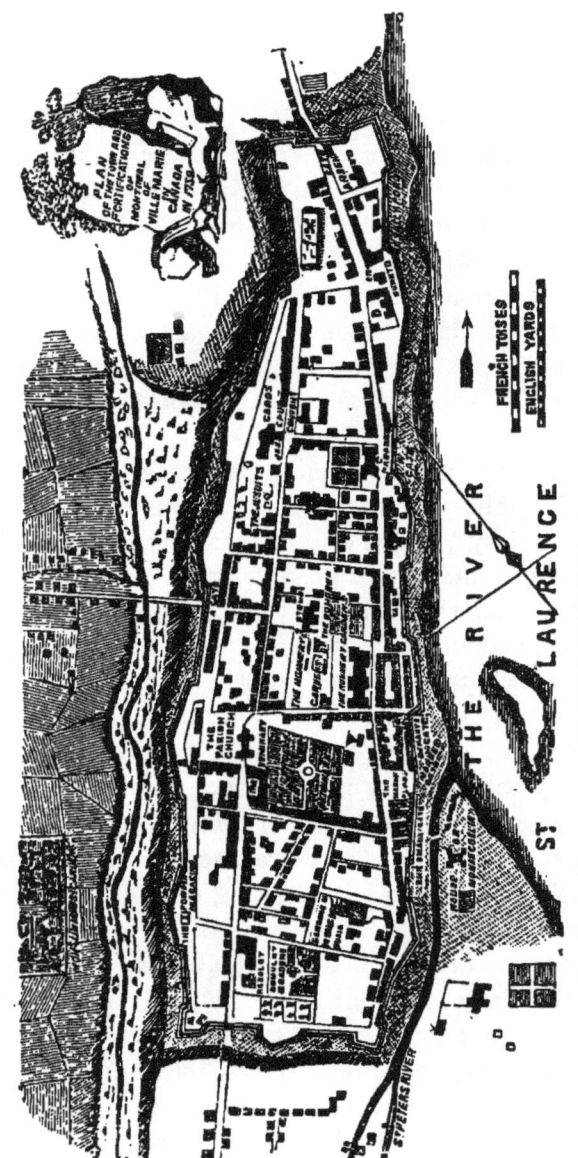

PLAN OF MONTREAL IN 1759.

"On the inside of the town is a cavalier on an artificial eminence, with a parapet of logs or squared timbers, and six or eight old guns, called the citadel. Such were the fortifications of Montreal, the second place of consequence in Canada, until the enemy raised the siege of Quebec; and then, in expectation that the English forces would follow them, a battery was erected, with two faces for nine guns, but had only four twelve-pounders mounted, two pointing to the navigation of the river, and the others to the road leading from Longue Pointe to the town, with a traverse for musketry, elevated on the inside of the battery, for the defence thereof, together with some piquet works, forming a barrier to the entrance of the place, with two advanced redoubts, were all the temporary works made for its defence.

"The inhabitants, in number about five thousand, are gay and lively, more attached to dress and finery than those of Quebec; and from the number of silk sacks, laced coats and powdered heads that are constantly seen in the streets, a stranger would imagine that Montreal was wholly inhabited by people of independent fortunes. By the situation of the place, the inhabitants are extremely well supplied with all kinds of river fish, some of which are unknown to Europeans, being peculiar to the lakes and rivers of this country. They have likewise plenty of black cattle, horses, hogs and poultry; the neighbouring shores supply them with a great variety of game in the different seasons, and the island abounds with well-tasted soft springs which form a multitude of pleasant rivulets."

## THE AMERICAN OCCUPATION IN 1775.

### *Montgomery—Franklin—Arnold.*

At the outbreak of the Revolution, it was natural that attempts should be made to enlist Canada on the side of the other colonies. The British traders seem, as a body, to have been willing, and at first many of the French also sympathized. General Philip Schuyler invaded the province by Lake Champlain, but falling ill, was replaced by the ill-fated Montgomery. Colonel Ethan Allen was despatched against the city, but on the 25th of October was taken prisoner, and thereafter sent to England. Soon Montgomery appeared; Governor Sir Guy Carleton, having an exceedingly small force, withdrew to Quebec, and the citizens capitulated On the 13th of November, 1775, at nine o'clock in the morning, he marched in by the Récollet Gate, and took up his headquarters in the large house on the corner of Notre Dame and St. Peter Streets, inhabited by a merchant named Fortier. There a tablet is placed, reading: "Forrêtier House. Here General Montgomery resided during the winter of 1775-6."

The house at that time is said to have been the largest and most magnificent in the city. The principal rooms were wainscoted all around up to a certain height, and, above that, tapestried richly with scenes from the life of Louis XIV. Over the principal door is to be seen the date "1767," underneath a niche intended for a statuette of a saint.

Generals Wooster and Benedict Arnold followed Montgomery in possession, the latter proceeding to his death in the gallant attempt to scale the defences of Quebec. In the meantime, the Commissioners of Congress, Franklin, Chase and Carroll, as already related, came to the city and brought with them its first printer, Fleury Mesplet. They were compelled to retire before Carleton, their army and cause having become unpopular with the priests and people, and reinforcements having arrived from England.

### Dorchester.

The brave character and the other services of Carleton, afterwards raised to the peerage under the title of Dorchester, are commemorated in the inscription at the corner of Dorchester and Bleury Streets: "This street was named in honour of Sir Guy Carleton, Lord Dorchester, commander of the British forces and preserver of the colony during the American invasion, 1775-76; twice Governor of Canada, and by whom the Quebec Act, 1774, was obtained."

### De la Corne.

Another officer who distinguished himself in the same campaign was De la Corne, a member of a good old French-Canadian family, the site of one of whose dwellings, either on St. Paul Street, opposite the west corner of Custom House Square, or on Bonsecours Street, is to receive the following: "Here lived the Chevalier Luc de Chapt, Sieur de la Corne and de St. Luc. Sole survivor of the shipwreck of the *Auguste*, 1761. Served with distinction in both the French and English armies. He exercised a great influence over the Indian tribes. Died 31 March, 1817."

The reference to the *Auguste* is to a ship which sailed for France with the greater part of the French *noblesse* who had decided to leave the colony. It was unfortunately wrecked, and all on board lost except De la Corne. The Bonsecours dwelling has just been taken down.

### Du Calvet.

A notorious adventurer and scamp of the same period was the Swiss Du Calvet, a man of extraordinary plausibility and facility with voice and pen, but who has of late years been conclusively proved to have been false simultaneously to the British, the French-Canadians and the Americans. His rôle with each was that of a wronged patriot. His house stands on St. Paul Street, near the Bonsecours Market. A tablet is being erected here, independently of the Antiquarian Society, by Mr. L. J. A. Papineau.

### OTHER OLD HOUSES.

Other old houses of interest are the **Papineau House,** on St. Paul Street, near the Bonsecours; the **Marquis de Lotbinière House** (1797), on St. Sacrament Street, opposite the Montreal Telegraph Company's office; the **Sir John Johnson House,** in the East End; the **McCord House,** in Griffintown.

Louis Joseph Papineau was the eloquent leader of the French-Canadians at the period of their rebellion of 1837–8: Chartier De Lotbinière was a king's engineer under Montcalm; Hon. John McCord was the leader of the mercantile British party who inclined towards the American Revolution.

On the Papineau House the legend is: "The Papineau House. Six of their generations have dwelt here."

The De Lotbinière mansion is tableted as follows: "Residence of the Marquis de Chartier de Lotbinière, Engineer-in-Chief of New France, 1755. He fortified Ticonderoga and Isle-aux-Noix. On his advice, Montcalm attacked Fort William Henry in 1757, and awaited the English at Ticonderoga in 1758."

An exquisite little specimen of the rich merchant's residence of an earlier period is the house on St. Jean Baptiste Street, occupied by the St. George's Spice Mills. It was probably built about 1680, by a trader named Hubert *dit* Lacroix. The handsome parlours and their carved-wood mantelpieces, the lofty warehouse room adjoining, the quaint hall and stairway, the curious, elaborated fireplace in the basement, and the high walls of the court-yard, are well worthy of notice by any permitted to see them. A tradition represents the house to have been the residence of one of the Intendants, but the assertion is disputed.

The oldest building in Montreal is possibly one owned by Mr. James Coristine, and situated at the rear of his fur establishment on St. Paul Street, just west of St. Nicholas.

It is claimed to have been built in 1666, and the vaulting is to-day perfect and solid and the walls very thick. The dwelling doubtless consisted of a low living-story, above the vaults, and was reached by stone steps in a square tower behind. Though much altered, the building retains traces of its early shape above.

Another quaint·erection stands next door, with gable

on St. Nicholas Street. On its yard face a small image-niche and window give a picturesque appearance.

*The McTavish Haunted House.*

This grim tradition has probably been hitherto the Montreal story most circulated among the English-speaking population. In 1805, Simon McTavish, the principal founder of the North-West Company, built a great house on the side of Mount Royal, upon the present property of Mr. Andrew Allan. He died before it was quite finished, and as it was left deserted, in a lonely situation, tradition had it that he had hanged himself in it. Dreadful sounds, particularly a horrible gurgling as if breath, were thereafter heard within by those who passed. On the tin roof, in the light of the moon, spirits were seen dancing. Few persons would approach, far less anybody inhabit it, and the mansion gradually fell more and more into decay and disfavour.

A form of the legend was that the proud North-Wester built the house preparatory to the coming of his family from Scotland; that his wife, a high-spirited woman, objected to coming out to a rude new country, but the husband hoped to surprise her upon her arrival by the presentation of a beautiful and well-appointed home; that one night, as the house was near its completion, some mysterious impulse moved him to visit it (for he lodged meanwhile at a farmhouse in the neighbourhood), when, just as he entered the basement and looked up, he saw in the moonlight her inanimate form dangling from the roof-tree. Though he knew she was in Britain, the apparition was so realistic and striking, that all work upon the house was suspended; and, sadly enough, when the ship which had been expected arrived, it brought news of her suicide by hanging in the garret of her old home, at the very hour when he had seen the apparition. He became a cynic, wasted and died, while the house, finding no purchaser, remained a sad and forbidding relic. It was of stone, and had a circular wing at each side. In the park, near the upper reservoir, a stone pillar covers McTavish's remains.

### *Améry Girod.*

Few know that under the cross-road made by Guy and Sherbrooke Streets sleeps a suicide. Yet it is true that Améry Girod, a Swiss, who took part as a leader in the rebellion of 1837, was buried there in pursuance of the old custom of interring a suicide under cross-roads. On the collapse of the rebellion, he had been hidden at a house in the country, and hoped to escape. The troops, however, found him, and were surrounding the house. He ran out and attempted to get away by creeping along a stone wall, but was shot—in the leg, I think—while doing so. He then killed himself with his sword, to avoid being hung. They buried him as just stated.

### THE TRAFALGAR LEGEND.

This story, of a lonely hermit of the Mountain, who, through madness of jealousy, had slain both his lady and her lover, is too long to tell here. He haunts a certain old garden-tower in the grounds of "Trafalgar," a residence on the Cote des Neiges Road, immediately above the Seminary wall, where his mysterious footfalls have been heard quite lately. The reader is referred to *Canadiana*, March, 1890, for the full tale.

### LA PLACE ROYALE.

Since the writing of the description of Custom House Square, its name has been changed to " La Place Royale," on petition of the Antiquarian Society, in order to mark the 250th anniversary of the foundation of the city by re-conferring on the locality the name given by Champlain. The writer and two other members of the Society, on the morning of the 18th of May, 1892, baptised the Square with St. Lawrence water, after removing the old signs and confiscating them as trophies. Mr. John S. Shearer stood godfather, the Secretary (Frank Langelier) poured out the water from a glass goblet, and I did my part by pronouncing the words.

### THE HOTEL DIEU PICTURE.

The legend of Ethan Allen's daughter and the painting of St. Joseph, narrated in connection with the Grey Nunnery, should have been attributed to the Hôtel Dieu. It is in the entrance to the cloister chapel of the latter, and is a large painting of the Holy family in an antique gold frame. It was once the altar-piece of the old Hôtel Dieu Church on St. Paul Street, now removed.

# INDEX.

# INDEX.

Aboriginal Traditions, 2
Algonquins, 2, 3
Agouhanna, 7, 106
American Occupation, 138
Amherst, Sir Jeffery, 34, 52, 91, 126
Arnold, Benedict, 54
Allen, Fanny, 81, 144
Anahotaha, 110; Death of, 113

Bell, the Great, of Notre Dame (Le Gros Bourdon), 12, 28
Bullion, Duchesse de, 22, 79
Bonsecours Church, 28, 67
Bank of Montreal, 32
Bonsecours Market, 58
Bourgeoys, Marguerite, 67, 93
Burton, 130

Champlain, Samuel de, 3, 8, 21, 23, 50, 104
Commerce, 11, 12
Cadillac, 12, 118
Custom House, 21
Compagnie de Nôtre Dame de Montréal, 105
Compagnie des Indes, 37
Churches, 33, 60
Callières, 24, 25, 35
Closse, Lambert, 26, 109
Carmelites, 95
Citadel Hill, 36, 39
Charlevoix, Père, 36
Canadian Pacific Railway, 12
Canadian Pacific Rail'y Bridge, 15
Château de Ramezay, 37, 53
Château de Vaudreuil, 38
Cemeteries, 51
Capitulation Cottage, 52
City Hall, 53
Court House, 55
Christ Church Cathedral, 62
Catalogne, 121

Canal, First, 121, 122
Conquest, 126
Clubs, 97, 100

Detroit, Founder of, 12
Du Luth (Du Lhut), 12, 118
Dauversière, Le Royer de la, 22, 79, 104
Dollier de Casson, 30
Dollard (Daulac), 111
D'Ailleboust, 119
De Beaujeu, 125
Demons, 103
Dorchester, 139
De la Corne, 139
Du Calvet, 140

Earthquake, the Great, 114

Fraser, Simon, 12, 134
Fortifications, 34, 136
Franklin, Benjamin, 54
Fort de la Montagne, 89

Gates of the City, 34, 39. 115, 136
Grand Trunk Railway, 12
Grey Nuns, 80
Gage, 129
Girod, Améry, 143

Hospitals, 76, 77
Hochelaga, 2, 5, 6, 7, 8
Hurons, 2, 3, 5
Henry, Alex., 12, 133
Harbour, 13, 15
Heavysege, Grave of, 52
Hôtel Dieu, 78
Hunt Club, 99
Houses, Old, 140

Iroquois, 2; Four Burnt, 117
Iroquet, 3

Iberville, 120
Irving, Washington, 131

Jacques Cartier, 2, 7, 8, 37, 48, 105
Jacques Cartier visits Hochelaga, 5
Jesuits, 36, 69
Johnson, Sir Wm. and Sir John, 130

Kondiaronk, 122

Lalemant, Père, 3
La Salle, 12, 117; Dwelling, 117
La Mothe Cadillac, 12, 118
Lachine Canal, 14
Laprairie, Battle of, 16
Longueuil Castle, 16, 122
Le Ber, Jeanne, 94
Le Moyne, 119
Longueuil, Baron de, 120
La Prairie, M. de, 121
La Vérandrye, 123
La Friponne, 125
Legend of Devil and Wind, 29
Legend of St. Père's Head, 109
Legend of the Red Cross, 20, 82
Legend of P. Le Maistre's Handkerchief, 108
Little River, 20
Legend of Hôtel Dieu Picture, 82
Le Maistre, Père, 108
Lévis, 129
MONTREAL—
    Site of, 2
    Aboriginal Name, 103
    Leading Characteristics, 11
    A Seaport, 12
    History of, 13
    Population, 13, 17
    Foundation of, 21, 107
    Earliest Church, 28
    In 1666. 134; in 1770, 135
Maisonneuve, Paul de Chomédy de, 23, 25, 31, 48, 67, 107, 119
Maisonneuve Statue, 25
Montreal Amateur Athletic Association, 97
McTavish Haunted House, 142
Montgomery, Headquarters of, 138

Mount Royal, 3, 6, 7, 9, 44
Mance, Jeanne, 22, 23, 79
Monks, 94
McGill University, 8, 13, 84
Mackenzie, Sir Alex., 12, 133
Molson, Hon. John, 14
Manor House, the First, 25
McGill, Hon. Jas., 37, 85
Montcalm, 38, 39, 123
Monklands, 194

Nuns of the Congregation, 93
Nôtre Dame de Montréal Church, 12, 26
New Orleans, Founder of, 12, 120
North-West Company, 33, 131
Nelson's Column, 37
North-Westers, 48, 131
Nôtre Dame de Victoire, 68
Nôtre Dame de Lourdes, 72

Ononchataronons, 3
Olier, Abbé Jean Jacques, 21, 104
Old St. Gabriel Church, 64

Post Office, 33, 55
Parks, 44
Palace of the Intendants, 124
Population, 13
Pilote, 24, 26
Pillory, 37
Public Buildings, 53
Printer, the First, 54
Près-de-Ville, 125

Récollets Church, 28, 72
Rocky Mountains, Discoverer of, 123

Seminary of St. Sulpice, 12, 25, 29, 30
Shipping, 13
Steam Navigation, 13
Schools, 89
Societies, 95
SQUARES, 8, 9, 21, 23—
    Custom House (La Place Royale), 20, 144
    Victoria, 33

# INDEX.

La Place d'Armes, 25, 129
Viger, 35
Champ de Mars, 35
Jacques Cartier, 36
Place des Jésuites, 36, 115
Dalhousie, 39
Dominion, 40
St. Louis, 43
Phillips, 44
St. Helen's Island, 10, 50
St. Lawrence River, 11, 16
St. Peter's Cathedral, 41
St. George's Church, 43
Synagogue, the First, 75
Streets, Naming of the, 115
Sports, 97
Skating Rink, Victoria, 99

Trafalgar Legend, 143
Towers, the Old, 90
Trappists, 94
Theatres, 97, 99
Tutonaguy, 106
TABLETS, HISTORICAL—
Hochelaga, 8
Molson, 14
First Public Square, 20
La Place Royale, 23
Founding of Montreal, 23
Fort of Ville-Marie, 24
Callières, 25
Manor House, the First, 25
First Parish Church, 28
Old Parish Church, 28
Seminary, 30
Nôtre Dame de Victoire, 68
Récollets Church, 72
Dollier de Casson, 30
Place d'Armes Battle, 31
Second Grant of Land, 32
Fortifications, 33
Beaver Hall, 33
Récollets Gate, 34
Charlevoix, 36
Place des Jesuites, 36
Jacques Cartier, 37
His Landing-Place, 105
McGill's Residence, 37
Château de Vaudreuil, 39

La Citadelle, 39
Château de Ramezay, 54
Old Christ Church, 63
Hôtel Dieu, 80
Mance, 80
The Towers, 91
Amherst's Camp, 91
Congregational Nunnery, 94
La Salle, 117
Du Lhut (Du Luth), 118
La Mothe Cadillac, 118
D'Ailleboust, 119
Le Moyne, 119
Iberville, 120
Bienville, 120
Schoolmaster, First, 121
De Catalogne, 121
Lévis, 123
De Beaujeu, 125
Amherst's Camp, 127
Capitulation Cottage, 127
Murray, 127
Closse, 110
Trudeau, 110
Dollard, 111
Johnson, 130
Burton, 130
Gage, 129
Henry, 133
Mackenzie, 133
Fraser, 134
Tecumseh, 134
Montgomery's Headquarters, 138
Dorchester, 139
De la Corne, 139
Papineau House, 141
De Lotbinière House, 141
McCord House, 141

Universities, 84

Vaudreuil, 122, 128
Ville-Marie, 94
Victoria Bridge, 14
Vimont, Père, 23, 103

Windsor Hotel and Hall, 42
Wolfe, Last Order of, 130
Y.M.C.A., 41

## PRINCIPAL AUTHORITIES CONSULTED.

Parkman, Sandham, " Rélations des Jésuites," De Belmont, Faillon, Lovell's Hist. Census for 1891, S. E. Dawson, *The Canadian Antiquarian, Hochelaga Depicta*, Mercer Adam's "The North-West," Dollier de Casson, Vie de Mlle. Mance, Vie de M. Olier, *Canadiana*, P. S. Murphy, Judge Baby, Gerald E. Hart, the late Roswell C. Lyman, B. Sulte, R. W. McLachlan, J. P. Edwards, De Léry Macdonald, M. Bibaud, Garneau, Champlain, Jacques Cartier's "Voyages," Lévis' "Journal and Lettres," Jodoin and Vincent, Brymner, Morgan, Kingsford, Tanguay, Beaugrand and Morin, and others.

Mr. Wm. McLennan contributed assistance of a unique sort—results of a systematic sifting made, for the first time, of the old notarial and other earliest archives of the city. To him are due the identification of the De Catalogne, LeMoyne, Du Luth, Laprairie, La Salle and Cadillac houses. His service to the public in thus contributing these facts should not be underestimated.

The writer desires to add that this little book being put together in haste, he is conscious it must contain inaccuracies and imperfections. In particular the Maisonneuve statue and some of the historical tablets quoted are only in process of erection, and may be slightly altered before their completion. Hasty and faulty as it is, however, it will, in helping to popularize a good deal of rare information, fill for the present a place which remains yet to be perfectly filled.

To some, it may appear singular than an advocate in active practice should put together a book of the kind. The author was induced to do so by the view that the historical tablets, which are a pet scheme of his, could only be rendered effective by an explanatory handbook such as the present; and when, therefore, the publishers proposed the matter, he accepted.

www.ingramcontent.com/pod-product-compliance
Lightning Source LLC
Chambersburg PA
CBHW020250170426
43202CB00008B/300